The Author

Thomas Jackson was educated at Downside School and Cambridge University where he read History before joining the Benedictine Community at Downside in 1958. He studied philosophy at Downside and theology at Fribourg University in Switzerland. In 1985 he left Downside and is now married and a full time writer living in Lancashire. As a young theology student at Fribourg he was appalled, at the time, by the irrelevance and waste of opportunity involved in studying highly abstract Medieval ideas in Latin - why can't we do something relevant to the nineteen-sixties for goodness sake? - but now, forty years later, he sees this time of exposure to the great mind of Aquinas as one of his life's most precious gifts. His interest in *The Origin Of Species* has been quickened by the realization that Aquinas would have loved Darwin just as he loved Aristotle. The idea of *The Origin* as a great loss to religion rather than an alternative to it is now a central pre-occupation.

Darwin's Error

The Poet Who Died

Thomas Jackson

four o'clock press

Dedication

I would like to dedicate this book to dear Downside
where I learnt so much, and especially to
Aelred Watkin and Philip Jebb,
great educators both.

Acknowledgements

I wish to thank Peter Harvey for editing my manuscript, Jag Lall for his cover design and Michaela Unterbarnscheidt at Discovered Authors for her unfailing courtesy, encouragement and patience.
I would also like to thank Caroline Jones of Osprey Indexing for her work on the index.

La gloria di colui che tutto move
per l'universo penetra e risplende
in una parte piu e meno altrove

(The glory of him who moves all things
Penetrates the universe and shines out
More in one thing and less in another)

Dante: *The Divine Comedy, Paradiso, Canto 1, verse 1*

'….. instead of thinking and learning to understand
nature, they break at once into the childish cry
'Design! Design!'…..The ignorance of the Kantian
philosophy is principally responsible for this whole
outcast position of the English.

Arthur Schopenhauer: *The World As Will And Idea*

Wie ich der Liebe abgesagt, alles, was lebt, soll ihr
entsagen!

(Once I renounced all the joys of love, so all living
things shall renounce them too)

Alberich, in *Das Rheingold* by Richard Wagner

'I believe from what I have seen Humbolds glorious descriptions are & ever will be for ever unparalleled: but even he with his dark blue skies & the rare union of poetry with science which he so strongly displays when writing on tropical scenery, with all this falls far short of the truth. The delight one experiences in such times bewilders the mind,- if the eye attempts to follow the flight of a gaudy butter-fly, it is arrested by some strange tree or fruit; if watching an insect one forgets it in the stranger flower it is crawling over,- if turning to admire the splendour of the scenery, the individual character of the foreground fixes the attention. The mind is a chaos of delight, out of which a world of future & more quiet pleasure will arise,- I am at present fit only to read Humboldt; he like another Sun illumines everything I behold. – '

Charles Darwin

Contents

Introduction

This book looks at Charles Darwin's *The Origin Of Species* and *The Descent Of Man* from what is perhaps a slightly unusual angle. My theme is that Darwin made one of the greatest discoveries in all of science, but at the same time presented it in a highly mythologized and misleading way. As far as I know, nobody has considered *The Origin* both as science and myth. Contrary to what is normally thought, the great majority of Victorian scientists did not accept natural selection, and in his later life even Darwin himself had considerable reservations about it. The discoveries of the true age of the earth and Mendel's laws of inheritance, which together in the twentieth century resoundingly rebutted the doubts about Darwin's theory, were still unknown in the nineteenth. Yet the public adopted natural selection with great enthusiasm. Despite the hullabaloo of 1859 the Church rapidly accommodated itself to Darwinism, and the theologians never used the doubts of the scientists to undermine natural selection, as they could so easily have done. How are we to explain this?

My answer is that societies validate themselves to themselves by creation myths. This has traditionally been one of the major functions of religion. Because the Victorians were exploiting nature in a way that had never been done before they had a special need to seek such validation, but the authority of religion was rapidly weakening as a result of German Biblical criticism and the new science of geology. They therefore turned to the authority of science. An account of origins that was scientifically unimpeachable, yet at the same time highly vulnerable to being mythologized, suited them extremely well. They wanted to be told not only that better adapted forms survive differentially in changing environments, but that there is an agency external to the organisms themselves that drives progress forward by ruthless extermination, just as Paley's had done by benign design. They wanted to believe that the conditions of their own society, leading to the triumph of the strong and the extermination of the weak, are inescapable laws of nature. In fact this external agency was, as Darwin presented it, just as mythological as Paley's had been, but was immensely persuasive because it appeared to be part of the science.

My first chapter discusses the need that societies seem to have to deceive themselves, the function that religion has so often fulfilled as a court of mythic permission in the provision of such deceptions, and why, in these logics of delusion, creation myths are of especial importance. For centuries Europe had proclaimed its belief in Christianity, while at the same time subverting the teaching of the founder of its beliefs to justify the very things that he had condemned. In the nineteenth century this prolific source of moral duplicity was weakening alarmingly. Chapter two discusses the difference between facts and meanings in science. The first can be validated, the second cannot. This is the crucial distinction that I bring to my understanding of *The Origin.* Chapter three explains why the Whigs, to whom Darwin's family belonged, were in acute need of a scientific theory that would validate their social and economic policies. Chapter four examines the major intellectual influences on Darwin, especially Locke's teaching that behind the deceptive world of sensation there is a true world of law discoverable by science, and Herschell's and Whewell's scientific methodology: (1) the assembly of facts (2) the inductive detection of regularities, or empirical laws, in the facts, and (3) the discovery, through deduction, of the truly explanatory laws, the *verae causae*,[1] that explain the empirical laws. The great example of this methodology was Newtonian physics. It was fatally misleading when it was applied to biology. Chapter five is devoted to Darwin's tendentious use of metaphor, and his presentation of natural selection as if it were a biological version of a Newtonian law of nature, which was in fact a misconception, in language that, extraordinarily, suggests not so much a law as a god. In chapter six I discuss the mythical qualities of *The Origin* and why the Victorian public took it so much to their hearts. In chapter seven I argue that *The Descent Of Man* functioned as a mythical justification of imperialism just as *The Origin* had been used to justify industrial capitalism.

* * *

In the subsequent, and final, three chapters I try to approach my subject from a slightly different angle. In chapter eight, *A Slow Dying Amongst Barnacles,,* I argue that Darwin never presented in *The Origin* the nature that he had actually encountered during his voyage in *The Beagle*. The outstanding feature of the journal that he kept on the voyage is his intoxication at nature's glory and wonder, recorded by one of the greatest prose poets in the language, but none of this made it into *The Origin*. During the two decades in between his marvellous adventure and the publication of *The Origin* this most wonderful man died emotionally. It is surely one of the greatest tragedies in the history of science. The key thing that we need to remember about *The Origin* is that it was written by a man with a crushed heart. Darwin needed to impress a scientific establishment that had little use for glory and wonder. Both they and he had an extremely narrow attitude to science that had been shaped philosophically by Locke and Hume. If Darwin had been as influenced by Kant as he was by Locke and Hume, we would, perhaps, have had the much greater Humboldtian work that *The Origin* might have been. Darwin's wonderful discovery that all life emanates from a single source would better have led him to stress the brotherhood of all life, not extermination and competition. His philosophical blindness to form warped his vision. He stressed nature's cruelty but, he of all people, forgot its beauty. If he had been influenced by the Kantian account of teleology he would surely not have committed so diminishing an oversight. He also failed to appreciate, too, the ever intensifying inwardness that has been the driving force of evolution. Again,

Kant would have saved him. Instead he substituted for it a highly mythical external agency that was in fact, ironically enough, a secularization of Paley's cosmic designer.

The Origin is as confused as it is because Darwin's heart was at war with his head. His heart had been enchanted by Humboldt but his mind had been shaped by Locke. *The Origin* is as it is because in this conflict the heart was totally overwhelmed by the head. If one of the pillars of Darwin's insight was the variations occurring within organisms, the other was that organisms are shaped by their environment. Both of these were influences originally emanating from Goethe that reached Darwin through Humboldt – though perhaps an infusion into the bloodstream of his experience rather than a direct illumination of his mind - a Kantian debt that *The Origin* in no way acknowledges. Darwin took up the environmental side of this equation and used it to develop his great theory, albeit in a highly mythologized way. But the other side of the equation, the inner variations, he neither investigated, though he frequently lamented his inability to do so, nor developed. The question that Goethe had constantly asked and the one that Humboldt when he was a young man insistently pressed upon him – why are natural things so beautiful? – he did not address at all. The empiricist tradition in science has always regarded such a question as outside its remit. But natural things are not only observable and measurable and spatially extended and mobile. They *are* beautiful. Why? English science's lack of interest in this question was Darwin's profound misfortune. The great Humboldtian companion to Darwin's *Origin,* the flowering of his heart that, perhaps in other circumstances, this great master of English prose, this most sensitive of men and most poetic of souls, would have given us, remains to be written.

(Endnotes)

1   It is surely wrong to use a Latin term where a simpler English one will do. But in this case *vera causa* is a technical term for which there is no substitute. The emphasis is on the purely logical deduction of eternal unchanging laws underlying and governing external phenomena, that are not directly observable in the phenomena themselves.

Chapter 1
Courts Of Mythic Permission

There can be little doubt that human beings are prone to act far more irrationally when they are part of a collective than when they are on their own. Individuals frequently quarrel with the neighbours who are living next door, but it is unusual that they come to blows and even more unusual that one neighbour actually kills another. Yet on the collective level we can find example after example of people banding together and suddenly turning on neighbours with whom they had lived peaceably for years, and slaughtering them with the most horrible and indiscriminate cruelty. Turks slaughtered thousands of Ottoman Christians in 1915. In the nineteen thirties Germans started to turn on Jews and ended by killing six million of them. In 1947 in India hundreds of thousands of Muslims were put to death by Hindus, in some cases taken off trains and torn to pieces in the most horrible way, and vice versa. In the nineteen nineties formerly close neighbours started killing each other in what had until recently been Yugoslavia, the gruesome massacre at Srebenica in 1995 being only one of numerous horrible examples. Khmer Rouge communists killed middle class people whom they had known for years in Cambodia, simply because they betrayed the fact that they were educated by wearing glasses. Hutus rose up against Tutsis and slaughtered defenceless women and children in thousands. In the 1970s in Argentina and Chile people denounced other people they had known for years to the torturers and death squads. During the Cultural Revolution in China university professors were hunted down and sometimes killed by their own students. Human beings can indeed be far more brutal than any brutes.

Yet when we examine these terrible events we always find that, far from their perpetrators regarding them as crimes for which they should feel guilt, they are always done for apparently good reason, usually indeed for the highest of motives. The Hutus rose against the Tutsis because they had been persuaded that if they did not do it the Tutsis would do it against them. In their own eyes the Nazis did not kill Jews because they enjoyed bullying people, or to get hold of their property, or even to take revenge for the part the Jews were held to have played in bringing about Germany's defeat in the first world war, but for a far more sacred cause, that of purifying the blood of their race. What a pity, said Himmler, addressing an audience of SS officers in 1943, that the extermination of the Jews will never be generally known, for it is one of the most glorious pages in our history. If you want to send sixty million people to the gulag, then you can be sure that it is for the most elevated of reasons, that of establishing a socialist paradise. Torturers who on occasion felt squeamish in Chile and Argentina were re-assured by military chaplains that they were carrying out a noble duty, protecting Christian truth against the scourge of communism. The Cultural Revolution was carried out in order to re-establish the purity of Maoist doctrine. Hindus killed Muslims and Muslims Hindus because they were the wrong religion, a reason that on many occasions in history has given licence to the most ferociously vindictive passions. In other words, as the human capacity for committing terrible evils increases so markedly on the collective level, so too on that level the need of those who perpetrate such things to deceive themselves about why they are doing what they do becomes correspondingly greater, and the methods by which they achieve such deceptions the more potently, and often subtly, effective.

With the advent of language the human capacity to deceive increased immeasurably, for it now became possible to give a false account of what was not immediately happening before the observer's eyes. One most effective technique societies use is to take the teachings of some great man and then turn them into their opposite, while fervently proclaiming devotion to his doctrines. This happened to both Newton and Adam Smith, as I shall argue later. Freud was another thinker whose ideas have been turned inside out. His vision of life was profoundly tragic, and his purpose was to free mankind from those primitive drives and passions that reduce peoples' rational control over themselves. He thought, above all, that he was trying to make people free enough from their animal nature to take responsibility for themselves. 'Where there was It there must become I' he wrote. But his purpose has been turned into its opposite. He has been widely taken as meaning that we should, on the contrary, use his techniques to free ourselves from any guilt and anxiety that might hinder our surrender to animal passions. Far from taking responsibility for themselves, people believe that Freud showed them that it is their parents they should blame for their misdeeds and their inadequacies.[1] The prize for misreading the source of their own inspiration must surely go, however, to the followers of Jesus Christ. The moral and intellectual legerdemain required for turning the teachings of a prophet who exhorted his followers to love their neighbour into a reason for burning him alive, must, in one dreadfully appalled sense, command one's admiration. For present purposes, however, I shall confine myself to discussing other ways in which whole societies deceive themselves with the greatest efficacy.

A yet more effective way whereby human beings deceive themselves, in order to evade the natural feelings of pity and the demand for justice that nature implants in them, is that of getting permission to over-ride these natural impulses from an unimpeachable supernatural source. This has been one of the major functions of religion all down the ages. There have been few great crimes committed by humanity, up to the twentieth century at any rate, that have not been blessed by some god. I shall give three examples. My first is that of Ashurnasipal II, who was King of Assyria from 883 to 959 BC. Even by the standards of those times Ashurnasipal was unusually cruel. Among the records of his reign we read:

'I built a pillar against his city gate and I flayed all the chiefs who had revolted, and I covered the pillar with their skin. Some I walled up within the pillar, some I impaled upon the pillar on stakes, and others I bound to stakes round about the pillar... And I cut the limbs of the officers, of the royal officers who had rebelled... Many captives from among them I burnt with fire, and many I took as living captives. From some I cut off their noses, their ears and their fingers, of many I put out the eyes. I made one pillar of the living and another of heads, and I bound their heads to tree trunks round about the city. Their young men and maidens I burnt in the fire. Twenty men I captured alive and I immured them in the wall of his palace. ...the rest of their warriors I consumed with thirst in the deserts of the Euphrates.'[2]

Needless to say, Ashurnasipal was particularly favoured by the gods. On another memorial, now in the British Museum, is written:

Ashurnasipal, vice-gerent of the god Ashur, chosen

of the gods Enlil and Ninurta, beloved of the gods Anu and Dagan, destructive weapon of the great gods, strong king, king of the universe, king of Assyria, valiant man who acts with the support of the god Ashur his lord. He has no rival among the princes of the four quarters, marvellous shepherd, fearless in battle, mighty… has no opponent, the king who subdues those insubordinate to him, he who rules all people…'[3]

My second example is taken from the fall of Delhi in India in 1857. The insubordinate sepoys had roamed the city and its environs looking for European victims, and had killed hundreds of British men, women and children. A relief force that had been sent to re-take Delhi had itself been besieged on a ridge above the city and had undergone terrible privations for many weeks, until it was re-inforced and the city was at last re-occupied by the British. Atrocious as the behaviour of the sepoys had been, the revenge of some of the British and those natives who had supported them was terrible beyond imagining. Thousands of Indians, many of them entirely innocent, were indiscriminately slaughtered. Villages were put to the torch and the men, women and children inside them burnt alive. Captured rebels were strapped to the mouths of canon and blown to smithereens by gunfire. Many, as a last insult, were smeared with pig fat, wrapped in pigs' skin and then hanged. The Reverend John Rotton, who had been chaplain to the relief force through all its privations on the ridge, forgetting that he was supposed to be the emissary of a teacher who had taught that you should forgive your enemies, exulted ferociously in these atrocities as the justice of God. In his thanksgiving sermon for the relief of Delhi he said:

'and now the counsels of evil men have been brought to nought, and every foul purpose of theirs completely frustrated, the triumphant army – the means which God had been pleased to employ in order to bring about these gracious ends – stood devoutly in the Divine Presence, ascribing unto Him praise, and saying glory and honour, power and dominion are thine'.[4]

There were few Anglican clergymen in either England or India who would not have said the same.

My third example is, by far, history's most skilled and successful practitioner of the art of declaring evil to be good in the name of God, and gathering benefit to itself in return for giving permission to secular rulers to commit crimes. I refer to the Papacy, for who else is more qualified for such a role than the Vicar of Christ himself? All through its history powerful worldly rulers have prostrated themselves at the feet of popes and craved such permissions, often showering gifts upon their benefactor in gratitude and thanksgiving. Here are some examples. Pepin wished to steal the crown of the Merovingians. The Pope blessed this unjustifiable theft and in return Pepin gave him the papal states. Charlemagne seized an empire by the sword. The Pope declared it to be both Holy and Roman and was given sorely needed aid against Constantinople as a reward. William the Conqueror had only the flimsiest claim to the English crown. But the Pope legitimized his proposed conquest in return for rich endowments to the Church of wealth and lands. William thought the Pope's support so important he even flew the Papal flag at the battle of Hastings. Henry II asked and received the Pope's permission to invade Ireland – for the Pope was supposed to have suzerainty over all small islands - thus inaugurating a thousand years of sorrow. The Albigensian crusaders pillaged, murdered and burnt alive with clear consciences because Innocent III had granted them a crusader's indulgence, not only legitimizing their seizure of heretics' lands but guaranteeing they would go straight to heaven in return for their pious services to the Church. The Portuguese invaders of the African Gold Coast in 1450 were so anxious to get permission to enslave their newly conquered subjects they actually fooled the Pope, Nicholas V, into believing that these peoples were muslims so that they could get permission to enslave them, because at that time the situation of unbaptized heathen was uncertain while papal decrees had established beyond doubt that muslims could be enslaved.[5]

The Spanish conquerors of the Americas were equally anxious to enslave the Indians to work the gold mines, so they asked, and received, from Alexander VI in May 1493 a similar permission. The Spaniards' problem was that even the Pope could not be fooled into thinking that South American Indians were muslims. So they requested and received a new act of papal *plenitudo potestatis*[6] making it clear that all pagans could be enslaved, provided it had been established that they were enemies of Christ. The Spanish therefore adopted the *Requirimiento,* developed by the jurist Palacios Rubios. On coming across a new Indian tribe a document was read out to them *in Spanish* informing them that the Pope had given their lands originally to King Ferdinando and now to his daughter Queen Joanna, with, thoughtfully appended, a long explanation of the temporal power of St Peter and the Popes as developed by Cardinal de Susa in the thirteenth century. They were then invited to declare their belief in the Lord Jesus and the Blessed Virgin. If the bewildered Indians did not accept baptism at once they were declared enemies of Christ and immediately enslaved. In time however, refugees from tribes unfortunate enough to have already been offered the graces of Christian conversion by the Spaniards began to inform their neighbours of these procedures, and the Indians learnt to accept Christianity with alacrity, starting to convert in alarmingly great numbers. The disgruntled Spaniards were forced to fall back on Aristotle's doctrine that some men are slaves by nature.[7]

In 1773 the European colonial powers, enraged by the humanity and justice so shamingly evident in the Jesuit missions in South America, demanded that the Pope abolish the order. In return for the secular powers using their influence on his behalf in the conclave that elected him pope, Clement XIV obligingly did so.[8] The Vatican concluded a concordat with Hitler, even though its nuncio to Germany, Eugenio Pacelli who later became Pius XII, could see Nazi atrocities taking place before his very eyes. According to John Cornwell, Pacelli played a major part in assisting the Nazis to come to power by effectively muzzling their only real rival, the Catholic Centre Party. In return for this favour he hoped that Hitler would allow the Vatican to appoint German bishops, which the Centre Party was resisting. Since Hitler intended to destroy Christianity anyway once he had got through the Jews, though he did not tell Pacelli that, he was only too ready to concur.[9] John Paul II made an official visit to Chile in 1987 and, on the occasion of Pinochet's golden wedding in 1993, a telegram was sent in the Pope's name conferring on him a special apostolic blessing.[10] Such resolving of the moral scruples of secular rulers has been a historic function of the Papacy of incalculable importance. To say that you believe in loving your neighbours and forgiving your enemies, and then to give permission for atrocities that have permanently disfigured and distorted human history in the name of your belief, is a moral and logical reversal so complete it requires an absolute *plenitudo potestatis* to accomplish it. If the lord of love and forgiveness himself, speaking so authoritatively, through his vicar, says it's all right, you can be assured it is.[11]

By far the most important, however, of all these strategies of self-deception is that of adherence to false myths. Myths are of great utility because it is of their nature that they cannot be disproved. But it is for another reason that they are of such extreme importance. They direct the human imagination, and it is the imagination that is at the centre of all that we do. It is the fundamental condition of all our experience. The physical world, looked at as a purely physical phenomenon, is actually composed mostly of empty space randomly punctuated by energy events appearing and then disappearing back into the void whence they came. But this is not how we experience it. The world we know is one of contiguous space and colour and solid objects moving forwards in time. It is the imagination that has turned the physical world as it is known to physics into the extraordinarily different experiential world as it is known by us. Nor did we evolve to know the world in the way that a physicist might. From the point of view of survival in a very dangerous world peopled by hordes of predatory animals, it was not adaptive for early human beings to work out intellectually every time that they were about to step on a snake whether or not this was a reptile of the dangerous kind, what the statistical chances were of surviving snake bites, or whether it would be better to prudently retire or try to arrest the snake with your primitive spear. Far more lives were saved if you saw the snake, then quick as a flash imagined what it might do to you, and then took evasive action propelled by algorithmic instincts. You jump out of the way. Similarly, it was of crucial importance to early man to be able to imagine that a lion might be behind a rock, even though he could not see one, rather than having to wait until he was actually confronted with it. It was far more adaptive to early man that he thought like a poet rather than like a nuclear physicist, and since we are all the genetic descendants of our remote ancestors, still today we react to the world primarily and far more easily in imaginative rather than intellectual terms, even though to us nuclear physics presents far greater dangers than do poisonous snakes.

From an evolutionary point of view mankind is a most extraordinary contradiction, so extraordinary that the attempt to explain the development of the human mind entirely in the same terms that have proved so fruitful when applied to the rest of evolutionary biology seems to me to be quite unsatisfactory (a topic that cannot be handled here). Biology has shown us indisputably that we are part of the animal kingdom, and only to be explained by evolution from more primitive animal forms ancestral to ourselves. We are wholly mammalian, we are directed by instincts and algorithms as are other animals, and genetically are virtually identical with those in the lineages most closely related to us. Yet our intellects differentiate us from any other beast as totally as an angel might be separated from a worm. Chimpanzees only think about their immediate environs and their immediate projects. Our minds can range over the whole universe and even speculate as to what is beyond that. Explaining this remarkable capacity as the consequence of early human beings outwitting and cheating each other in order to get more sex does not seem to fit this bill. Given that the intellectual and animal sides of ourselves are so different as to be almost incommensurable, and yet mind and body are so intimately related they must be not just different parts of us but in some sense the same thing, what wondrous faculty is it that holds these two aspects of our nature in relation to each other? It is the imagination. The imagination takes the deliverances of sense perception which, in so far as they are as yet only excitements of nervous tissue can be explained in wholly physical terms, and turns them into pictures that we can think, know and understand. It is the imagination that holds these two sides of us together and makes us into whole persons.

Everything we do we first imagine and then do it. Even so simple an act as opening a window you picture to yourself before you do it – I'm going to get up, walk over there, pull down the catch and pull back the glass pane – though in such ordinary everyday actions our preliminary acts of imagination are so habitual and so instantaneous we hardly notice them. You never or almost never, however, go to open the window in a completely neutral frame of mind. It is never a purely intellectual exercise, but one that is motivated by, underpinned, shot through and impregnated with emotions and feelings. You go to open the window because you *feel* it's stuffy in here. You go to open it with feelings of glad anticipation because you will be in a more immediate contact with the garden that you have so carefully tended and love so much. Or you go to shut it because, yet again, the next door neighbour's adolescent's pop music is blaring so loudly it has become unbearable. You feel yourself boiling with anger. Because our actions are always performed within the matrix of the imagination they are always coloured by emotions and feelings. You imagine how lovely it is going to be when you throw back the casement and smell the freshness of the garden. You imagine the tortures to which you would like to subject next door's teenager. On the collective level these emotional colourings that underpin and guide action are what myths are about.

Myths are extremely condensed symbolic summaries of the fundamentals of our engagement with the world, and it is for that reason that they are so intensely charged with feeling. We work out intellectually how we are going to achieve our goals. But we adopt the goals themselves for reasons that belong not to intellect but to feeling. We go abroad on holiday, using our minds to work out how to get there, because we *feel* we need a break. We take on a new job because it will enable us better to house and feed the family we love. We go to fight a war and learn how to fire a rifle because we have deep feelings of patriotism for our country. Myths are emotionally highly charged because they compress all these profound and complex feelings into a very small symbolic space. They condense the background reasons, so complex and so involved, of why and how we have come to be living our lives the way that we are, into a short story that enable us to grasp in an instant the history explaining us. They summarize our engagement with the world, and it is for that reason that myths are of such supreme importance in directing what we do, and spell our deepest motivations from the background of our conscious minds into the foreground.[12] We all have the story of who we are and where we have come from in the back of our minds directing what we do.

* * *

Imagine a man living in the southern United Sates who has a gun, passionately believes in his right to defend himself, is a fundamentalist Christian and believes in capital punishment. Then 9/11 happens. It is unlikely that he will coolly appraise whether or not this is a trap set just for people like him, or whether it would be best to make a complaint to the United Nations and leave it at that. His engagement with the world is such it is far more likely that he will spell out, without even considering alternatives, a conviction that these evil-doers, these invaders of his land, should be condignly punished. 'Once upon a time people were oppressed and trampled upon by tyrants but some brave men set sail and found a land of freedom, where they self-reliantly defended themselves and their families and even today…'. Here is another example. Some highly committed liberals somewhat surprisingly supported the decision taken by the US and British governments in 2003 to go to war in Iraq. Since this was a war that, from one point of view, you could easily have portrayed as a neo-colonialist intervention, you would perhaps expect such liberally minded persons to be at least ambivalent about the issue. But some were not. I would guess that much of the reason was that they felt that tyranny should be overthrown, and that in the wake of 9/11 the values of the enlightenment were under attack and religious fanaticism must not be allowed to triumph. I doubt very much whether most of them weighed up all the purely strategic and political advantages that might accrue from invading Iraq and came to the conclusion that it was the right thing to do. Far more likely, their perception of themselves as people carrying the banner of the enlightenment was what counted, all the complicated reasons why the overthrowal of tyranny and obscurantism is such an important thing compressed into a myth. It is this myth that carries their fundamental beliefs from the background of their minds, where it normally resides, to the forefront and spells out their engagement with the world, and it is this that decides them to favour the option of going to war. 'Once upon a time people lived in darkness but some brave men defied the witch-doctors and their dark superstitions and started to live by the light of reason, and even today…' We all have a precious story in the back of our minds that encapsulates our deepest and most passionate beliefs about who we are.

Myths reach further back behind our personal history into much remoter periods. They reach right down into the deeply buried roots of feeling that evolved during the extremely distant ages when mankind was still a hunter-gatherer on the savannahs, touching emotional triggers that have come down through all the chromosomal generations even into our genes today. It is for this reason that we still dart back in instantaneous panic if we see a snake, although the likelihood of stepping on a poisonous snake in Basingstoke or Peterborough is small, and for this reason too that we have woven into our mythologies countless stories pointing out the dangers of snakes. Mythic symbols reach far down into these deeply buried darknesses and make them available to our conscious minds. But unconnected symbols do not mean very much to us. It is only when they are embedded in coherent narratives that our minds can grasp their significance. Fearing your father and desiring your mother on the one hand and forgetting things on the other, for example, do not seem immediately to be very connected. It is only when we read the story of Oedipus that we come to understand how important it was that his parents had abandoned him when he was an infant, and it was his own father he had killed at the crossroads and his own mother whom he had inadvertently married without realising it, and only then that we are brought to see the connection. It is because myths reach back to such profound beginnings that the most important of all myths, and those by which we are most profoundly and completely able to deceive ourselves, are creation myths. Creation myths always give the impression that they are about the creation of the world. But they are not. They are always about the mystical origins of a people. They always tell us how the gods created the world *in order that our social group could dwell in it.*

Here are three examples. My first example is a

Navajo creation story. According to this account the Navajo emerged from three previous peoples who had dwelt in underworlds before entering into a fourth, the Glittering World. The previous three peoples from the underworlds were half- animals, half-insects (how myths get these things right) or masked spirits, as they are still recalled in Navajo ceremonies. The First Man and the First Woman came out of the Black World, as did Spider Woman who taught the Navajo women how to weave. These three met in the First House (the Hogan) as Talking God had told them to, and there they created the four sacred stones that mark the boundaries of the Navajo homeland. After setting up the boundaries they went on to make the sun and moon, but Coyote stole the stars and scattered them all over the sky. The Holy People then made the clouds and the rain. They made the four clans of the Navajo, the Near Water People, the Mud People, the Salt Water People and the Bitter Water People.

My second example is a Mande creation myth from West Africa. In the beginning there was only Mangala, the Singular Powerful Being. Mangala made a seed hoping it would grow into the world but it didn't. So he took two twin seeds and this time he succeeded. He thus began the dual gendered twinship that is essential to Mande culture. But one of the male twins, Pembo, tried to escape from the egg that the twin seeds had grown into. Pembo stole a piece of the womb's placenta and out of it he made the earth. He then tried to re-fertilize what was left of the womb by committing incest with it. In order to save what was left of his creation, Mangala decided to castrate and kill Pembo's brother, Farro, so that he could resurrect him from the dead. Mangala took the rest of the placenta and made the sun from it, thus condemning Pembo to darkness and night. Pembo and Farro both had children and this is the origin of the exogamy that characterizes Mande society today.

My third example is a Maori creation myth. Io, the supreme being, created Ranga, the Sky Father, and Papa, the earth mother. They had many children, but they lay on top of them so that the children could not see the light. The children grew to resent this, so they decided to separate them. Tane put his feet on the earth and with a tremendous heave tore Ranga apart from Papa. They bled profusely and this is the origin of the red ochre that is so sacred to the Maori today. But there was one thing still missing, so they went to their mother Papa for advice. She told them to travel to Kwia-uku where they would find some clay. They did this, and out of the clay they made the first woman. This shows that it is not woman that makes man, as you might think, but man who made woman. Thus we see why it is that man is superior to woman. [13]

In all these stories the only people ever mentioned are the ancestors of the tribe whose creation myth this is. The places mentioned are always those known to the reciters of the fable. The rituals and customs of the tribe are established as sacredly given from the beginning of time, and are therefore irreversible and immune to rational criticism or reform.

Although these stories have become localized and particularized they have clearly been handed down from very remote periods through many generations, and have sufficient features in common to make it likely that they originate from a very early time indeed, before the scattering of peoples took place. They are attended with intense emotion, and their recitation during sacred rites of renewal, generally during new year ceremonies when the creation of the world is re-experienced and celebrated, evokes strong feelings of group solidarity. It is through such evocations that primitive tribes strengthen social bonds and re-affirm the collective identity of the group. It is hardly surprising that such strong emotions should be called forth by these myths of the beginning, when we consider the conditions under which the first human beings must have lived. In the nineteen-sixties the prevailing theory explaining the success of human evolution was that of Man the Hunter. Promoted by Raymond Dart and Robert Ardrey, the thesis maintained that man came first in the race because he was the most savage and ruthless of all the predators. Violence is bred into our genes.[14] This thesis has now been almost entirely exploded. C.K. Brain, re-examining skulls with holes in them that Ardrey and Dart had taken as evidence of human intra-specific violence, showed that the holes neatly fitted the gap between the lower canines of a leopard. This and similar evidences made it clear that early man, far from being the great hunter, was an extremely vulnerable prey. Barbara Ehrenreich, in her book *Blood Rites,* speculates that early humans must have crossed the savannahs in troupes organized very much like those adopted by baboons today.[15] Baboons keep a marching order with the females and infants at the centre of the group protected by the big males, while the young males occupy the extremely dangerous outer peripheries. Such troupes annually lose a up to quarter of their young males. To fall behind the group is fatal. A sick or wounded baboon will struggle so desperately to keep up with the troupe it often neglects to eat, thus weakening itself still further. To fall behind the troupe is to be eaten 'within hours of the troupe's passing and probably before its heart stops beating'[16].

* * *

If life on the savannah is still so dangerous today, how much more must it have been in the Pleistocene when Africa was swarming with predatory animals. Human beings only survived because of intense group solidarity, which over-rode the tendency to selfishness that both genetic theory and daily observation confirm is so frequent a human behaviour. Early humans, however, had one advantage that baboon troupes do not. We know from the size of their skulls that their brains must already have been remarkably large, and therefore there is every reason to suppose that they were as capable of identification through imaginative imprinting as we are. Strong feelings of group loyalty encoded in highly compressed symbols must have united such early groups, and once there was language these symbols could have been communicated in narrative form. In *The Creative Explosion* John Pfeiffer speculates that ice age art was almost certainly connected with intitiation ceremonies.[17] The sparse evidence of food remains and of utensils in the deepest parts of the cave indicates that they were only rarely visited. On the cave walls are sometimes found engravings of shaman-like figures wearing masks, clearly for some ritual purpose. The famous 'sorcerer' from the cave at Les Trois Freres, with staring eyes and reindeer horns, is crouching as if in a dance imitating an animal. The cave at Niaux contains over 500 footprints, all so small they must have belonged to children or adolescents. There are similar footprints at Tuc d'Audubert, but here the evidence is even more striking, for the footprints fan out in a regular pattern, as if that of a dance.[18]

Sound as well as sight must have been an important part of these ceremonies. Many paintings have been placed at just those points in the cave where the acoustic resonance is most striking. Pictures of men beating drums and the remains of primitive flutes show without question that music as well as visual art was an important part of the rituals held deep in the caves. Pfeiffer argues that the caves were deliberately chosen for initiation ceremonies because they were strange and frightening. Measures were taken, as among aboriginal tribes today, to impart the tribe's sacred myths, the means by which it transmits an intense sense of imaginative identification to a new generation, through ceremonies that were designed to impress themselves unforgettably on the memory and imagination. If the model of present-day aboriginals can be used reliably, it was mythical creation stories that were at the very centre of these ceremonies of group renewal. If there is truth in these speculations, then initiation into secret knowledge of creation myths was so important to primitive ice age people they went to the lengths of penetrating into the deepest parts of underground caves, and decorating them with engravings and portraits that can only have been placed where they are with the greatest difficulty. Creation myths were at the very centre of their perception of themselves and their place in the world. It is to our peril if we imagine that in our enlightened scientific age so important a need for such deep imaginative imprinting has not also descended to us. Human beings establish social bonds by orientating themselves imaginatively round tribal myths, especially creation myths. That is the way we evolved.

Myths of the beginnings sometimes not only explain why a particular people come to be living in their own land but also justify their occupation of somebody else's, or their usurpation of other peoples' property. Even more effectively than gods and popes, they act as courts of mythic permission. Thus in Indo-European mythology the first cattle raid was conducted by the first warrior, whose name was Third. According to the myth, cattle had been given by the creators of the world, a priest called Man and a king called Twin, to the Indo-Europeans, but they were stolen by a monstrous three headed snake whose name was Serpent. Third set out to recover the stolen cattle, and began his quest by enlisting the aid of a warrior god to whom he offered libations of intoxicating drink. Fortified both by the intoxicant and the help of the god he recovered the stolen cattle. This was obviously justified, as the cattle had originally belonged to the Indo-European people, had been given to them by the creators of the world in fact, and had been stolen by their enemies, i.e. the Neolithic inhabitants of Old Europe. Throughout Indo-European history Third remained a model for warriors who cast themselves in his image - raiding and plundering and killing convinced the while that they were engaged in a sacred duty. According to Bruce Lincoln this myth is one of, if not *the,* most important narratives in world history, for it provided the ideological impetus and justification for the Indo-European conquest of Europe and Asia; it is the imperialist's myth par excellence.[19] One of the interesting features of the myth is the part that the intoxicant plays in it. It seems to imply in a backhanded way that Third accomplished his feat while he was in an irrational state. This ability to turn things on their heads, and to delude themselves through myth that what is irrational and unjustifiable is valid was an outstanding feature of the Indo-European mentality. The Scythians justified their domination of their neighbours, the Agathyrsia and the Gelone, by a myth which told how the eponymous ancestors, Agathyrus and Gelonus, had failed in a mythic contest of strength to string Herakles' bow, whereas the ancestor of the Scythians had succeeded. This use of myth to manipulate natural feelings of sympathy, fairness and justice, is among the most important features of human behaviour.

Another myth of this type is that recounted in the

Biblical Pentateuch. We commonly think of the Biblical creation as recounted in the first chapter of Genesis, but in fact the whole of the first five books are about the creation of the Jewish people by Yahweh. They are entirely justified in taking the territory of the Moabites and the Amalekites and the Hittites from them because Yahweh has promised it to the children of Israel, and there is never any question that they will not succeed, because God is with them. This myth is, of course, exceptionally interesting because it so obviously has relevance to the tensions in the Middle East today. Even the most secular of Israelis, and there are large numbers who are either agnostics or atheists, feel with the profoundest passion that they have a right to dwell in the land of Israel. This is not based on philosophical arguments or on historical or legal quibbles about the validity of the Balfour Declaration. It is a deep visceral feeling, even certain knowledge would not be an inappropriate phrase, born to them by the myth of their origins. The constant attempts by well meaning liberals to bring about compromise by getting both sides to understand the justice of the other's case, with appeals to principles of humanity, justice and fairness are, as is all too evidently the fact, doomed to failure. In all creation myths land is intimately bound up with the creation of the tribe. What they teach is that the land *is* the people. Appealing to Lockean principles of human rights is like asking the parties to commit suicide. Attempts to bring about peace will make little progress until this all-consuming visceral identity of tribe, history and land is understood. Western negotiators would do far better to try to get the Israelis to look more closely at their own creation myth. For what we have here, in the Old Testament, is the most remarkable of all creation myths. A myth that at the beginning is as irrational, chauvinist, unjustifiable and unjust as any we could find anywhere, flowers into the great universal vision of Isaiah. Israel is to become the light of the nations and is to love a God who cares not just for Israel but the far-off coast lands. Israel's true promised land, according to Isaiah, is not a Palestine riven by hatred but the whole world united by love.

If myths are such tightly condensed narratives of feeling, and if they operate so far below the level of thought, how can there be false myths, and still less true ones, since truth and falsity are judgments made by the intellect? It is true that myths are not rational in the sense that the theorems of Euclid are. But we have to remember that we are intellectual as well as imaginative creatures. What we need to learn to do is to define what our own myths are, in our case especially no easy task, and to learn to stand aside from them and bring them to the bar of rational judgment. Is our own myth leading us into irrational and unjust behaviour, does it benefit us and does it benefit others, is it the richest and most helpful source of satisfaction that we can find? Can we absorb into it other peoples' creation myths, so that we come not merely to tolerate them but to profoundly understand and sympathize with them? One of my aims in this book is to attack the idea, so common in industrialized western society, that since we live by science we are immune to being led astray by mythic fantasies and are therefore superior to, and more rational than, those who are.

I shall spend the next chapter arguing that there is a distinction in science between facts and their meanings, and because of this, especially in a society where so vital a distinction is so consistently overlooked, far from being immune, science is highly vulnerable to being mythologized. Furthermore, because its particular myth is that it is not a myth, its mythologies are especially irrational, insidious and dangerous. In particular I want to re-examine and de-mythologize the great sacred text of western liberalism, *The Origin Of Species.* My quarrel with Darwin is that, having made his great discovery that evolution can be explained in wholly natural terms and needs no mythologically invoked external creator god, he then re-religionized and re-mythologized his own discovery, replacing the fictional deity he had dethroned with another that was even more unhelpful and misleading. I hope I can persuade you that *The Origin Of Species* was not only a great work of science but, equally importantly, it was the creation myth of the modern world. Genesis was not overthrown so much by scientific argument as by a rival myth.

The great problem for the Victorians was that their science was increasingly showing them that the myths by which mankind had traditionally lived, in their case the Biblical Genesis, were fallacious, and yet, although they did not commonly realise it, for evolutionary reasons they as much as anybody else needed to organize their world view within a mythical matrix. The age-old capacity of religion to act as a court of mythic permission was rapidly weakening, so they needed to look elsewhere. They needed a myth that would bless their ransacking of nature. And in particular, like the Indo-Europeans and the Old Testament Hebrews, they needed a myth that would unimpeachably justify their acquisition of other peoples' possessions and land. The only solution was for science itself to perform the function of myth, but to do that successfully it had to pretend that it was not one. It is this feature that made Darwinism so exceptionally misleading. I hope I can persuade you too that, as myths go, Darwin's myth was far more fallacious and harmful than the one it replaced, and that it underlies many of our contemporary woes. The question is not whether we should replace mythology by science and reason, for, because of the way we evolved, we have no choice but to live by mythology. The question therefore becomes, which is the most helpful and rational myth we can live by? It is most definitely not the western liberal myth gripping tightly in its tentacles most contemporary rationalists.

(Endnotes)

1   See Bruno Bettelheim 1982 *Freud and Man's Soul* London Penguin

2   George Roux 1964 *Ancient Iraq* Allen and Unwin London. Penguin ed 1992 p.290

3   plaster of cast from Kalhu Assyria, now in British Museum 1901.19.0001A

4   William Dalrymple 2006 *The Last Mughal* London Bloomsbury p. 404

5   J.F. Maxwell 1975 *Slavery and the Catholic Church* pub.
    B. Rose. See also|Joel S. Panzer 1996. *The Popes and
    Slavery* Alba House. Panzer gives a version of Alexander VI's
    permission far more favourable to the papacy than Maxwell's.
    I do not wish to get involved in this controversy, my point
    here is the use that the Spainards made of the permission,
    which on any reading was misinterpreted, in order to appease
    their own consciences.

6   Literally 'fullness of power'. The doctrine was developed
    during the twelfth century in the investiture contest.
    From the time of Gregory VII onwards the popes began
    to claim that all authority, even that of the Holy Roman
    Emperor, ultimately emanated from them and could only
    be exercised with their permission.

7   David E. Stannard 1992 *American Holocaust.* Oxford OUP
    pp 63-66

8   Eamon Duffy 1997. *Saints And Sinners* Yale Nota Bene ed.
    2002 pp. 245-6.

9   John Cornwell 1999 *Hitler's Pope* London Viking

10 See J-J. Tamayo-Acosta *Pinochet's Men In The Vatican.*
    Also Karl Backman *About Five Popes.* Both available on
    the internet. The telegram to Pinochet was actually
    sent by Cardinal Sodano, the Vatican Secretary of State,
    with a handwritten note by John-Paul enclosed.

11 In spite of my dismay at the behaviour of the popes I am,
    nevertheless, a believing Catholic, though the reader
    might perhaps be forgiven for feeling confused, and
    wondering how I can possibly go on believing in an
    institution that has characteristically behaved so badly
    during so much of its history. We can, however, distinguish
    the office from those who have performed it. I believe that
    there is some sense, anyway, in which the popes are
    successors of St Peter and the rightful heads of the Church.
    We should therefore respect them and listen most
    carefully to the guidance that they give, even if we do not
    always feel called upon to follow it. Not all popes have
    behaved badly and some have taught wisely. The uproar
    about Paul VI's decree on contraception in *Humanae*

Vitae, for example, blotted out the encyclical's extremely beautiful teaching on marriage, perhaps one of the best documents on human sexuality, if we leave aside the controversial contraceptive issue, in the twentieth century. Whatever his failings may have been, John-Paul II preached tirelessly against war. His campaign against the culture of death is surely something the modern world needs to listen to. To respect the office and yet deplore the way most of its officers have fulfilled its duties is not illogical. Although Christ promised Peter's successors his everlasting support, he didn't guarantee that they would behave well. Indeed, given his own experience of higher ecclesiastics during his lifetime, perhaps he didn't even expect it. Clearly this topic deserves a book. This is not it.

12 See Herbert Fingarette 1969 *Self-Deception* Routledge Kegan & Paul London. Univ of California ed. 2000

13 see www.magictails.com/creationslinks.html

14 Robert Ardrey 1961. *African Genesis* New York Dell

15 Barbara Erhenreich 1997. *Blood Rites.* London Virago

16 quoted by Erenreich from Pfeiffer John *The Emergence Of Man* 1972 New York Harper & Row

17 John Pfeiffer 1982 *The Creative Explosion* Cambridge Ms & London. Harper & Row

18 For footprints at Tuc d'Aubert see A. Marshack 1972 *The Roots Of Civilization* New ork McGraw-Hill p. 242

19 Bruce Lincoln 1981 *Priests, Warriors and Cattle* Berekeley. Univ of Cal Press.

Chapter 2
Facts and Meanings

My purpose in this chapter is to undermine that cherished foundation principle of the western liberal myth, the idea that science gives us certain truth. Infallible truth is never what science gives us. What it gives us are increasingly well verified hypotheses and increasingly less misunderstood facts. Truth embraces both fact and meaning. We can prove the existence of facts. But we cannot prove what they mean. We can only imagine their meanings, and that within the limited world picture that, at any given time, contemporary science reveals to us. In any given age, therefore, we inevitably misunderstand what the facts we know actually do mean, for the whole history of science suggests that future discoveries will radically alter our, at present, incomplete and temporary understanding of them. I am not therefore criticizing the Darwinians for misunderstanding the meaning of the facts that Darwin had discovered, but for misunderstanding that those facts were, especially to begin with, bound to be misunderstood.

I am taking many of my ideas here, that science does not give us certain absolute truths but only relative imaginary ones, mainly from two sources. One is Thomas Kuhn's book *The Structure of Scientific Revolutions.* There can have been few books written in the twentieth century that have been so widely read and so profoundly misunderstood. Kuhn did not think that scientific *facts* are uncertain. He did not think it possible that the scientists would one day find that, after all, the earth is flat. Nor did he think that the facts are only relatively true within scientific discourse. Nor that science is the mythical narrative of western capitalist culture. What he did think was that scientists understand the facts they discover within limited intellectual frameworks he called paradigms. Normally they do not question the paradigm within which they are working. They do what he called 'normal science', solving what he called 'puzzles', i.e. showing how facts which do not seem to fit easily into the paradigm can, in fact, be shown to do so. Thus within Ptolemaic astronomy the controlling idea that the heavenly bodies all go round in harmonious perfect circles was thrown into confusion by the discovery that some planets move backwards.

The conundrum was resolved by the thesis of epicycles, small circles within which the planets were moving which themselves were being carried round within bigger ones. Thus, even though within half of its epicycle the planet was moving backwards, in a much larger sense it was moving forwards. Belief in the paradigm was not only saved but actually strengthened by its perceived ability to explain even so apparently damaging a discovery. But as even more anomalies appeared, the paradigm of perfect geocentric celestial harmony could no longer be maintained and it collapsed in the face of the much better Copernican explanation. Science does not, according to Kuhn, advance inexorably and steadily by gradual accretion as item after item is added to the already existing canon, contributing yet one more brick to 'the great edifice of truth we know today'. Instead it proceeds by sudden and disorientating spurts that disrupt settled periods of stasis. When disturbing new facts appear 'normal scientists' go into ever greater intellectual contortions to accommodate the new facts within their world view until they can do so no longer, and at that point the whole framework of their understanding of the scientifically perceived world collapses, to be replaced with astonishing rapidity by another.

Another instance that Kuhn gives is the attempt by dyed in the wool Newtonians to reconcile their view of the universe with Einsteinian relativity. On this view Einstein cannot be used to show that Newton was wrong. It was possible, after all, to fly a man to the moon using no more than Newton's equations. In fact, Newton's equations can be derived from Einstein's own, in all situations where the velocity of bodies is small relative to the speed of light. In that sense Newton's can be shown to be a special case of Einstein's. But this apparent resolution disguises the much more fundamental divergence that whereas Newtonian mass is conserved, Einsteinian is convertible with energy. The very nature of the bodies themselves is profoundly different. Only at relatively low velocities does it happen that the two can be measured in the same way. Once you accept that mass and energy are convertible and time and space not absolute but relative, then the whole Newtonian view of the universe collapses and you move into a different paradigm. It is important to understand that Kuhn never said that paradigms are simply reflections within science of general social attitudes and conditions. His is a strictly scientific book. Nor did he say they were simply imaginary constructs. They are, instead, attempts to bring subordinate facts within the orbit of understanding generated by the major discoveries dominant in any particular scientific field at any given time. Nevertheless, Kuhn does show us that scientists understand their discoveries within intellectual frameworks that decisively modify the way they are understood.[1]

A thinker who *did* say that the scientific enterprise is essentially imaginative and that the imaginary frameworks within which scientists understand it are profoundly affected by social conditions was Adam Smith in his *History of Astronomy.* Scientific discoveries, according to Smith, are propelled by the three emotions of surprise, wonder and admiration. We are surprised when we come across something that disturbs the even tenor of the train of natural events to which we are used. We wonder how it can be connected with the rest of nature. Then – and this is the crux of Smith's argument - we set about *imagining* unknown factors that, if they can be verified, will show how the anomaly is connected to the rest of nature. Then *the entire natural sequence* will be once again *perceived* to be rational and harmonious. Thus scientific hypotheses are attempts to make imaginary connections between the phenomena of nature in such a way, according to Smith, that they can not only be verified but allay the sense of disquiet with which anomalous facts disturb the human mind. As imaginative hypotheses are verified, they move from the category of fantasy into that of theories confirmed by fact. But the theories themselves are not factual, they continue to be products of the imagination. Then new phenomena appear that again disturb us, so once more we are forced to imagine unknown factors that will relate them to the framework of understanding that we currently have. We are driven to imagine new explanations that will reconcile them with what we already know. In turn these new ideas may become verified and factually confirmed, but the verified facts are always cocooned, as it were, within a connecting outer shell of the imaginary, for yet more new facts will appear whose relation to what is already known has once more to be imagined.

People look for different kinds of connecting links in different ages. What they turn to science for is to give them a coherent view of the world in accordance with what they are capable of imagining at any given time. Thus at a time when mankind had very little control over nature men attributed thunder and lightning bolts to fairies and demons. In a later age they attributed them to 'the invisible hand' of Jupiter. In a still later more prosperous age they understood nature as a wholly harmonious system presided over by a benign God. 'Thus science gave birth to the first monotheism.' In a yet later and even more prosperous age the imagined 'connecting links' of which science is composed were seen to be not supernatural but natural. *But we easily mistake the connective hypotheses of science for nature itself.* So dazzlingly universal and so ubiquitously verified had the hypotheses of science become, in the age of Newton, that 'even we, while we have been endeavouring to represent all philosophical systems as mere inventions of the imagination, to connect together the otherwise disjointed and discordant phenomena of nature, have insensibly been drawn in, to make use of language expressing the connecting principles of this one, as if they were the real chains that Nature makes use of to bind together her several operations'.[2] Few more important statements have ever been made about science.

* * *

Adam Smith completes Kuhn's thought. He was right. There is a difference between the empirical facts that science discovers and the imaginary connecting links with which scientists attempt to relate them to each other. There is a distinction between facts and their meanings. And scientists do not imagine things, even in their own fields, in a vacuum. Generally, they imagine in the way that people imagine things in the age in which they live. Geniuses imagine even more, but originally and differently. Yet as science has advanced, so stunning have its empirical discoveries been we have tended to forget this, and confuse the way we view the phenomena with the phenomena themselves. This has been particularly damaging in the cases of both Darwinism and neo-Darwinism. In both of them the understanding of the facts has been greatly modified by the general social and intellectual conditions of the age and, in both cases, they have in turn strengthened and confirmed those conditions. I will try to demonstrate these ideas, that there is a difference between facts and their meanings, and that the particular connecting links with which scientists explain the facts are both imaginary and deeply affected by the general world-view of the scientists, by giving two examples.

My first example is Newton's discovery of the universal nature of gravity. Even now the elegance with which Newton's laws connect together so many disparate phenomena astonishes us. Yet they have been understood to mean completely different things. One version of their meaning was that held by the French mathematician Laplace. This was really the culmination of the admiration for the 'Newtonian mechanical universe' that was so widespread in the eighteenth and nineteenth centuries. Laplace was a typical, almost *the* typical, figure of the French Enlightenment. Because the universe was believed to be entirely rational everything could be understood by reason and reduced to rational order. Thus the revolutionary committees had attempted to replace the twelve months of the year by a more mathematically rational ten, and then give the months meaningful names that would reflect their seasonal characteristics, the hot one, the misty one, and so on. The different districts of France, which were divided from each other by wiggly boundaries reflecting a myriad accidents of history, were replaced by the perfectly square *departements* that still exist today. Laplace was the very incarnation of this spirit. Until the twentieth century he was probably the greatest of all investigators of celestial mechanics after Newton himself. He was one of the first to postulate the existence of black holes and gravitational collapse. He was a firm believer in total and absolute causal determinism. Nothing in the universe, even the smallest event, could happen by accident. In his *Essai Philosophique sur la Probabilite* he wrote:

'We may regard the present state of the universe as the effect of the past and the cause of its future. An intellect which at a certain moment would know all forces that had set nature in motion, and all positions of all atoms of which nature is composed, if this intellect were also vast enough to submit these data to analysis, it would embrace in a single formula the movements of the greatest bodies in the universe and those of the tiniest atom; for such an intellect nothing would be uncertain and the future just like the past would be present before its eyes.'

But this hypothetical vast intellect, which has become known as Laplace's demon, was the one thing he didn't think existed. In his system all intellectual and spiritual phenomena were reducible to a materialist explanation. On one occasion when he went to present his *Celestial Mechanics* to Napoleon, the Emperor playfully commented 'Monsieur Laplace, they tell me you have written this large book on the system of the universe and have never even mentioned its Creator'. Laplace replied 'I have no need of that hypothesis'. At which a bystander remarked 'Oh but it is a beautiful hypothesis. It explains everything'. 'It may explain everything', said Laplace, 'but it predicts nothing'. [3]

Now compare this interpretation of Newtonian mechanics with Newton's own. It is only in recent decades, with the publication of more of Newton's papers, that the role played by alchemy in his thought has been more fully realised. The conventional view of his time was that gravity was an extremely attenuated form of corporeal matter, dependent on the contiguous action of corpuscular particles upon each other. Against this background, the alchemical framework of his thinking was essential in enabling Newton to escape from this paradigm into understanding gravity as action at a distance. Whereas his contemporaries were working within a mechanistic structure, so much so that even animals were simply seen as complex machines, Newton's frame of thought was organic. For him inanimate material things were incomplete plants or animals. Whereas for Laplace gravity was a purely mechanical and rationally predictable force, for Newton it was the pneumatic body of Christ. For Laplace the universe was one vast mechanical system, for Newton it was a temple filled with divine fire.

His primary sphere of interest was not science as we think of it, but ancient esoteric knowledge and theology. He thought not only that every word in the Bible was, in an extremely sophisticated sense, literally true but also that it was a secret numerological code. He spent as much time studying these codes and working out from them the date of the final fall of the Great Whore of Rome and the second coming of Christ as he did studying gravity and motion. For Newton the esoterically alchemical and mathematically scientific aspects of his interest were inextricably linked. He regarded God as so utterly spiritual and transcendentally other, and matter in its native state as so gross, that for him the idea of the Incarnation was inconceivable. For this reason he was an Arian. He thought that Christ was not himself God, but the first of God's creations, a kind of cosmic demi-urge through whom the universe had been made. The most important idea that he derived from the esoteric writing of the ancients, especially from Hermes Trismegistus and the Stoics, was that of the Vegetative Spirit. The term came from the Latin *vegetare,* meaning to animate or enliven. Gross matter was like a kind of dough permeated by the Stoic *pneuma* or breath of life, which transformed it into ever higher and subtler and more ethereal organic forms. Even stones and rocks therefore were organic, in the most primitive meaning of the word.

'The earth is a great animal' Newton wrote 'or rather an inanimate vegetable that draws in aethereal breath for its daily refreshment and vital ferment and transpires again with gross exhalations.'[4] This cosmic aethereal breath was 'a subtle spirit', 'nature's universal agent, her secret fire', and the 'material soul of all matter'. Newton believed that this universal animating spirit came down daily from the divine throne and descended through all things in the form of gravity until it had reached the basest material things in the universe, and then ascended again to its divine source. He was immensely interested in ancient religious rituals. He believed that originally there had been a pure religion that had been lost, but is nevertheless to some extent preserved in fragmentary form in Judaism. From clues in the Bible and other ancient texts he believed that this religion had centred round what he called a *prytaneum,* a divine fire at the heart of the world. In the oldest form of religion the ancients represented the metaphysical structure of the world by 'a fire for offering sacrifices that burned perpetually in the middle of a sacred place.' The priestly processions of the Egyptians showed that their theology was based on the science of the stars, the Jewish priests processed round a fire on the altar and lit seven lamps to represent the planets. This *prytaneum* symbolized the cosmos, with the fire at the centre representing the sun and the space round it the whole world which was 'ye true and real temple of God & therefore that a Prytaneum might deserve the name of his Temple they framed it so as in the fittest manner to represent the whole systeme of the heavens'.[5] The whole universe was therefore a sacred temple, with the sun most especially the sacred seat of the divine. From it the Vegetative Spirit streamed down diurnally from the sun into the world through gravity, and returned through the ascending hierarchies of material things until it again went back to the sun in ever subtler manifestations of the ether. As an illustration of the different ways scientists can interpret the same data, the divergence between Newton and Laplace is staggering.

My second example is the so-called anthropic principle. The term was invented by a cosmologist called Brandon Carter at a symposium held at Krakow in Poland in 1973 to celebrate the 500th birthday of Copernicus. It was Copernicus who had first realised that the earth was not at the centre of the universe, but only a subordinate planet in the solar system. Subsequent discoveries that the sun itself was only one star among billions in the Milky Way, and the Milky Way only one among billions of galaxies, had made the earth seem peripheral indeed. Life, as Stephen Hawking put it in his vivid way, is 'only a chemical scum on a moderate-sized planet'. But in Carter's view the fact that the earth supports life makes it, perhaps uniquely, especially important. And not only that. For life to appear, so many unlikely conditions have to be fulfilled, all at the same time, its development has to be regarded as a virtual statistical impossibility. Already in 1957 Robert Dickes had noted that for life to develop the age of the universe had to be just right. If it were much younger there would not have been time for carbon to have been built by nuclear reactions within stars, if it were much older planetary systems would have come to an end.

To the age of the universe we have to add the even more unlikely condition that the strength of gravity has to be exactly right. Newton had discovered that gravitational force lessens in accordance with the inverse square of the distance between two bodies. But this is an essentially relative concept. It tells you nothing about the absolute strength of gravity. Since then scientists have worked out this absolute strength. For working purposes we can call it 6.673. For life to occur gravity had to be exactly of this strength. If it were weaker stars and planets would never have formed. If it were stronger the stars would all have collapsed into themselves long ago. But there seems to be nothing in the laws of physics that decrees that the strength of gravity has to be exactly 6.673. The same is true of the strong force within the atom. If it were different by only the slightest fraction, all the hydrogen in the universe would have turned into helium at a very early stage of the universe's existence and carbon could never have developed. The same is true for the constants of the other two forces in the universe, the weak nuclear force and electromagnetism. Their completely arbitrary values had to be just right. A whole host of other conditions also have to be met. How are we to explain this 'just-rightness' of the earth?

One explanation is given by the so-called weak anthropic principle (WAP). This states that the conditions for life must have occurred in the universe at least once, for otherwise we wouldn't be here discussing it. So obvious and tautologous a proposition arouses little opposition. Far, far more controversial is the strong anthropic principle (SAP). This states not only that life has happened in the universe, but must happen. This, of course, implies teleology, and than that there is no concept that more immediately arouses the suspicions of scientists. Nor is there agreement among those who accept the strong principle. Some scientists believe that eventually science will discover a Theory of Everything that will unite quantum theory with relativity and reduce the four basic forces of the universe to one. Perhaps it will then be seen that the numerical values of the constants are not accidental and arbitrary at all, but flow inevitably from the unified theory. But, of course, the problem here is that we do not have a theory of everything. For theists, the principle argues for a designer God. They see no other explanation for such fine-tuning. But others do. Many scientists accept the multiverse explanation. To non-scientists the universe we inhabit seems already to be far bigger than can be even envisaged. The idea of an infinity of universes is so incredible as to be meaningless. Yet there are extremely persuasive scientific arguments pointing in that direction. In an infinity of universes everything that is possible must sooner or later, and in some place or other, happen. Somewhere or other, therefore, life must occur. It so happens that we are in that time and place.

If the multiverse explanation seems to be beyond the bounds of comprehension, a fourth solution may well seem even more so. This is the future anthropic principle (FAP), presented by, among others, Tipler and Barrow in their book *The Anthropic Cosmological Principle.* This view rests on two concepts. One is that of the backward causation known to quantum theory. In ordinary experiential terms this makes no sense. Cause moves by definition from time present to time future. A conception that takes place during sexual intercourse, for example, causes a birth nine months later. But in the quantum world this is not necessarily so. It is as if the birth retrospectively causes the conception. The other concept is computational. All life forms process information, and therefore all organisms are, from one point of view, computers. Of these by far and away the most complex is the human brain. But it is not outside the bounds of possibility that an artificial computer could be built just as powerful and complex. Indeed, that is not just possible but probable, and that soon. According to Ray Kurzweil two streams of development are likely to reach climactic points co-incidentally in about 2030. In the area of neuro-science it is likely that by then the whole architecture of the human brain, all those millions of neurons and synapses, will have been completely mapped in the way that the human genome has now been unravelled. By the same date, and here Kurzweil invokes the so-called Moore's law[6] that computer power doubles every few years, computers will be powerful enough to match even this degree of complexity. Already the PC on your desk is many times more powerful than what it took to send a man to the moon.

By 2030 the complexity of computers will be equal to that of human beings. But once they reach this point, unlike human beings they will be able to design further generations of computers even more powerful than themselves. This process will be cumulatively self-promoting, and since in principle there is no reason why life (if silicon-based rather than carbon-based computation can be called life) should not last for millions of years into the future, there would seem to be no reason in principle why artificial computation should not eventually create a complete virtual universe which it could control. Laplace's demon will have finally materialized and become, if not flesh, at least whatever medium at this consummatory time has replaced silicon. At that point, or omega point as its evangelists call it, the principle enunciated at the very beginning of the information revolution by Alan Turing, generally regarded together with John von Neumann as the father of the computer, will become a reality: 'it is possible to build a universal computer: a machine that can be programmed to perform any computation that any other physical object can perform'.[7] Because they would be able to reproduce virtual versions of all physical processes, such a generation of machines would be able to make use of quantum principles of backward causation. They would thus be able to re-write the past, and manipulate the evolution of the universe in such a way that the earth became bio-friendly and began to follow a path that led eventually to themselves .

Needless to say such speculations have aroused fierce opposition. In a much quoted review of Barrow and Tipler's book Martin Gardner invoked the principle of The Completely Ridiculous Anthropic Principle (CRAP).[8] He was able to find no more withering form of ridicule than the last two sentences of Barrow and Tipler's own work: 'At the instant Omega Point is reached life will have gained control of all matter and forces not only in single universes, but in all universes where existence is possible; life will have spread into all spatial regions in all universes which could logically exist, and will have stored an infinite amount of information, including all bits of knowledge which it is possible to know. And this is the end.'

If facts are irrefutable, their interpretation is often a wilderness of speculations. It is because there is a distinction between facts and meanings in science that *The Origin* was able, at one and the same time, to contain a great factual truth enmeshed in a highly falsifying myth.

(Endnotes)

1   Thomas Kuhn 1970 *The Structure Of Scientific Revolutions*
    Chicago. Univ of Chicago Press
2   Smith Adam *Essays On Philosophical Subjects* Liberty
    Fund Indianapolis reprinted by Oxford Univ. Press 1984.
    p. 105.
3   I took much of my information about Laplace from the
    Wikiped entry on the internet
4   B.J. Dobbs 1991 *The Janus Faces of Genius: The Role of
    Alchemy in Newton's Thoughts.* Cambridge Cambridge
    University Press pp 24-52
5   quoted in Dobbs p.151
6   Paul Davies 2006 *The Goldilocks Enigma* London Allen
    Lane p.206
7   quoted by Davies *op cit* p.255
8   see Wikiped entry under *Anthropic Principle*

Chapter 3
Darwin: The Social Background

Charles Darwin was not the first Darwin to be an evolutionist. His paternal grandfather, Erasmus, was one of the earliest to believe and promulgate the dangerous doctrine with a vigour that earned him the title of the English Lamarck. A rumbustious figure from the eighteenth century, Erasmus was a huge man with appropriately large appetites for both food and women. If not an atheist he was next door to it, as perhaps befitted a member of the Lunar Society, a group of forward looking and freethinking midlanders, which met once a month to consider the latest scientific ideas, and included such luminaries as Joseph Priestley. He was also the Shrewsbury doctor. An expert on nervous diseases, he thought that many ailments of this kind, at least those afflicting the male of the species, could be alleviated by prescriptions of more sex. He tended to express his scientific ideas not in academic but in literary form, and his poem

Zoonomia was felt by many to express the spirit of the age far better than anything written by Coleridge or Wordsworth:

> *Organic life beneath the shoreless waves*
> *Was born and nurs'd in Ocean's pearly caves;*
> *First forms minute, unseen by spheric glass*
> *Move on the mud, or pierce the wat'ry mass…*

Darwin's father, Robert Waring Darwin, inherited Erasmus's Shrewsbury practice and was equally widely respected as a doctor. Like his father, Robert was a free thinking all but atheist. Unbelieving in Christianity, he was equally contemptuous of the Unitarianism of the Darwins' Wedgwood cousins, 'a feather bed to catch a falling Christian' as he called it. His secularism was, however, not unmitigated by prudence. His lack of Christian belief did not prevent him from proposing the lazy life of a country parson to Charles, when his son's ignominious failure to complete the medical course at Edinburgh had confirmed the father's view that there was now no hope of the son making any mark upon the world. He also advised Charles to conform outwardly and hide from a future wife any atheistical opinions that he might harbour, as atheism upsets women and mars marital harmony. Whereas Erasmus was one of the first evolutionists, Robert was among the first capitalists. He made a fortune out of shrewd money lending and canny investments in new industrial enterprises such as the Trent and Mersey Canal. Charles was thus reared on the incoming tide of the secular, Whiggish, entrepreneurial spirit of the new industrial age; a positivist middle class inheritance that was further augmented by his close connection on his mother's side with the wealthy pottery entrepreneurs the Wedgwoods, who lived only a few miles away. The bonds between the two families were drawn yet tighter by cross-cousin marriages, of which Charles's own was by no means the first. To understand Darwin, the first thing we have to grasp is that before all else he was in brain, breath and bone a middle class Whig.[1]

Rambling through the Shropshire countryside collecting natural specimens and conducting scientific experiments in what was a surprisingly sophisticated home made laboratory with his brother, the second Erasmus, Charles grew up quite insulated from the vast social upheavals that were convulsing England. The Industrial Revolution that was making Robert Waring Darwin rich was also reducing uncountable others to a hitherto unheard of poverty and misery. In 1811 the Luddite movement began in Nottingham, taking its inspiration from the mythical King Ludd who was supposed to have been the first to smash a stocking machine. Home hand workers, whose livelihood was imperilled by the new textile machines lately installed in factories, started wrecking the contrivances that were impoverishing them. The movement spread rapidly through the north of England before it was brutally arrested by the authorities. In a mass trial at York in 1813 the leaders of the revolt were sentenced to death by hanging or to transportation, although the sentences were commuted on appeal. Then in August 1819 a huge holiday crowd, many of them women and children dressed in their Sunday best, assembled at St Peter's Fields in Manchester to hear the famous radical orator Henry Hunt. Nervous of trouble, the magistrates read the riot act and sent the yeomanry in to disperse what its apologists later claimed was an entirely pacific crowd. To protect Hunt, his supporters linked hands to prevent the yeomanry from reaching the podium from which he was speaking, and at that point the magistrates ordered in the cavalry, ostensibly to protect the yeomanry. Eleven people were killed and four hundred injured. Hunt was arrested and sentenced to two years' imprisonment.

By the time Darwin departed England on his voyage in *The Beagle* tensions had grown greater still. By 1826 the plight of the handloom weavers in East Lancashire, put out of work by the post-war recession and Crompton's and Arkwright's new spinning and weaving machines, had become especially desperate. Statistics collected from Blackburn and Darwen in March 1826 showed that of 10, 686 weavers 6, 412 were out of work and 1,467 were working half time.[2] In his book *Rural Life of England,* published in 1838, William Howitt wrote:

'Everywhere extend wild naked hills, in many places totally unreclaimed, in others enclosed but exhibiting all the signs of a neglected spiritless husbandry; with stunted fences or stone walls; and fields sodden with wet from want of drainage; and consequently overgrown with rushes. Over these naked and desolate hills are scattered to their very tops, in all directions, the habitations of a swarming population of weavers. The houses are as free from any attempt at beauty or ornament as possible. Without, where they have gardens, these gardens are as miserable and neglected as the fields; within they are squalid and comfortless. In some of these swarming villages; ay and in some of the cottages of the manufacturing towns too, you can scarcely see a window with a whole pane of glass. In one house in the outskirts of Blackburn, and that, too, an alehouse, we counted in a window of sixty panes forty-eight broken ones, and this window was in a pretty uniform character with its fellows; both in that house and in the neighbouring ones. It is not possible to conceive a more melancholy contrast than that which the filth, the poverty and the forlornness of these weavers' and spinners' dwellings form to the neatness, comfort and loveliness of the peasantry in many other parts of the kingdom. As is generally the case, in the poorest houses were the largest families. Ten and eleven children in one poor hovel was not an uncommon sight......' [3]

* * *

The colliery owner William Hulton, giving evidence to the Emigration Commission in 1827, spoke of distress 'Which I could not have conceived to have existed in a civilized country'. He described the township of Westhoughton where half of the 5000 inhabitants were totally destitute:

> ' Mrs Hulton and myself in visiting the poor, were asked by a person almost starving to go into a house. We there found on one side of the fire a very old man apparently dying; on the other side a young man about eighteen with a child on his knee whose mother had just died; and evidently both the young man and the child were suffering from want; of course, our object was to relieve them, and we were going away from the house when the woman said, "Sir, you have not seen all". We went upstairs and under some rags we found another young man, the widower; and on turning down the rags which he was unable to remove himself, we found another man who was dying and who did die in the course of the day. I have no doubt that the family were actually starving at the time.' [4]

Like Hulton, some well off people were deeply moved by such sufferings. In Haslingden a group of ladies known as the Dorcas Society were extremely active in relieving the indigent, to the undisguised admiration of *The Haslingden Chronicle.* But such charities were rare. In late March 1826 the Blackburn Weavers' Union petitioned Peel, the Home Secretary, whose grandfather had been born in nearby Oswaldtwistle, to provide relief from public funds. 'Were the humane man to visit the dwellings.....of the weavers and see the miserable pittance...divided between the wretched parents and their starving little ones, he would sicken at the sight and blush for the patience of humanity.' The appeal fell on deaf ears. Even some of the manufacturers banded together to press the President of the Board of Trade, Huskisson, to introduce a minimum wage. Huskisson replied that theirs was 'a vain and hazardous attempt to interpose the authority of the law between the labourer and his employer in regulating the demand for labour and the price to be paid for it'. In the House of Lords the Prime Minister, Lord Liverpool, further exonerated the Government from responsibility: 'I am satisfied that government or parliament should never meddle with these affairs at all, but they do harm, more or less... On enquiry it would be found that by far the greater miseries of which human nature complained were at all times... beyond the control of human legislation'.[5]

Faced with such unyielding lack of concern, the desperate weavers took matters into their own hands. On Monday April 26th 1826 a large mob gathered in Accrington where they smashed twenty power looms. Moving onto Oswaldtwistle they smashed a further sixty looms in the Walmsley Brothers mill, and then in Blackburn two hundred in the Bannister Eccles mill. The mob had by this time grown to several thousand and troops sent to apprehend them turned back in dismay. Flushed with success, the next day the rioters moved on to William Turner's abhorred Middle Mill at Helmshore, where a further hundred looms were smashed, while troops in nearby Haslingden dithered. The next day proved to be the last. Moving on to Chatterton near Ramsbottom the mob was at last brought under control by a large military force sent from Bury. The aftermath now followed. Soldiers and police combed Lancashire arresting ringleaders, who were often denounced by government spies and informers who had attached themselves to the fringes of the crowd. Thirty five men and six women were sentenced to death, though in the event all these sentences were commuted to life imprisonment or transportation. Whereas the desperate pleas of the starving for government help had been met with a granite refusal, the factory owners whose looms had been damaged were compensated to the tune of £16,000, of which Turner alone received over £1000, paid out of the rates levied on already poverty stricken households.

* * *

These levels of suffering were not temporary occurrences in isolated pockets of the economy, such as that of the unfortunate handloom weavers, but were normal and endemic in early Victorian England. Engels' description of Little Ireland as it was called, only a stone's throw from where today the BBC offices are on Manchester's Oxford Road, in *The Condition of the Working Class in England* published in 1844, still holds us spellbound:

> 'Heaps of refuse, offal and sickening filth are everywhere interspersed with pools of stagnant liquid. The atmosphere is polluted by the stench and is darkened by the thick smoke of a dozen factory chimneys. A horde of ragged women and children swarm about the streets and they are just as dirty as the pigs which wallow happily on the heaps of garbage and in the pools of filth. In short, this horrid little slum affords as hateful

and repulsive a spectacle as the worst courts to be found on the banks of the Irk. The inhabitants live in dilapidated cottages, the windows of which are broken and patched with oilskin. The doors and the doorposts are broken and rotten. The creatures who inhabit these dwellings and even their darkest cellars, and who live confined amidst all this filth and foul air – which cannot be dissipated because of the surrounding lofty buildings – most surely have sunk to the lowest level of humanity. That is the conclusion that must surely be drawn even by any visitor who examines the slum from the outside without entering any of the dwellings. But his feelings of horror would be intensified if he were to discover that on the average twenty people live in each of these little houses, which at the moment consist of two rooms, an attic and a cellar. One privy – and that usually inaccessible – is shared by about one hundred and twenty people. In spite of all the warnings of the doctors and in spite of the alarm caused to the health authorities by the cholera epidemic, the condition of the slum is practically the same in this year of grace 1844 as it was in 1831.'[6]

Manchester was not alone as the host of these conditions. Robert Baker, a surgeon and factory inspector in Leeds, described cellar dwellings inhabited by Irish that he had visited:

'I have been in one of these damp cellars, without the slightest drainage, every drop of wet and every morsel of dirt and filth having to be carried up into the street; two corded frames for beds, overlaid with sacks for five persons; scarcely anything else in the room else to sit on but a stool, or a few bricks; the floor in many places absolutely wet; a pig in the corner also; and in a street where filth of all kinds had accumulated for years. In another house, where no rent had been paid for years by reason of apparent inability to do it, I found a father and mother and their two boys, both under the age of sixteen years, the parents sleeping upon similar corded frames and the boys upon straw on the floor upstairs; never changing their clothes from week's end to week's end, working in the dusty department of a flax mill and existing upon coffee and bread'.[7]

Every working class district of Manchester that Engels visited was much the same. It was how unnecessary all this filth and degradation was and how easily, but for the totally uncaring attitude of the well off, it could have been alleviated that disgusted him, even more than the desolation he describes. Houses were built higgledy-piggeldy as cheaply as possible, with no thought for the welfare of their occupants. It was the lack of a human order that appalled him, the invasion of reason by a chaos of unchecked exploitation. Even the builders would have profited more in the long run from better built properties, were it not that quick and easy profit was all that pre-occupied their minds. The utterly poor were vulnerable to unscrupulous shopkeepers, who made their wretched state still worse by adulterating victuals. Ale and porter were treated with *cocculus indicus,* a dangerous poison used as a cheap substitute for malt and hops. New beer had sulphuric acid added to make it taste mature. Flour was mixed with alum to whiten poor quality grades, and tea leaves mixed with used leaves treated with gum and then dried. [8] Prosecutions for such frauds were infrequent and desultory. Whereas punishments for the poor were immediate and severe, infringements of the law by the rich were usually treated leniently. Thus at Haslingden where the hated William Turner harshly fined his workers a day's pay for the slightest mistake or indiscipline in his mill, the highest fine imposed on a mill owner before 1850 was only £25, for employing twenty children for more than 58 hours a week.[9] This was hardly surprising as the magistrates were often the factory owners.

The vivid contemporary descriptions of the suffering in the north of England were matched by Cobbett's *Rural Rides,* chronicling the widespread distress in the south. As in the north, movements of rebellion were met with savage reprisals. After the southern Swing riots in the autumn of 1830 19 men were hanged, 644 imprisoned and 481 transported. Mayhew said that passing from the skilled artisans of the west end of London to the unskilled ones of the east was like entering a new land and encountering a different race.[10] It was the lack of concern of the rich for the poor, as if they were an alien species living on a different planet, that so astonished Engels. In 1831, when cholera broke out in Manchester, the authorities became alarmed that the disease might spread to the better off classes, and then indeed slums were cleared and the worst cellars filled with quicklime. Whether the poor who had inhabited them were forced to move to even more insalubrious dwellings Engels does not record. But as soon as the outbreak had passed these measures ceased. In Manchester 'the villas of the upper classes are surrounded by gardens and lie in the higher and remoter parts of Chorlton and Ardwick or on the breezy heights of Cheatham Hill, Broughton and Pendleton....these plutocrats can travel from their houses to their places of business in the centre of town by the shortest routes, which run entirely through working class districts, without even realising how close they are to the misery and filth which lie on both sides of the road'. This was because these broad thoroughfares were lined with shops that it was in the interest of the shopkeepers themselves to keep clean and presentable. Early Victorian England was a place where horror was unnoticed and where pity had died.

* * *

The land to which Darwin returned in 1836 was a very different place to the one he had left. The three-cornered struggle for the control of England between the old Tory landowners, the new Whig middle classes and the desperate poor had now entered a new and even more intense phase. During *The Beagle's* voyage the Reform Bill extending the voting franchise had been passed in 1832, and a Whig government elected which had passed its flagship bill, the Poor Law Amendment Act, in 1834. Malthusian and Benthamite ideas were now to be put into practice. For the greatest good of the greatest number the harsh laws of Ricardian political economy were to be followed uncompromisingly, the Malthusian doctrine that charity shown to the poor would only make their condition worse by encouraging them to breed yet more profligately, harshly applied. The old Elizabethan Poor Law had thrown responsibility for looking after the indigent upon the local parish. It distinguished between the deserving and the undeserving poor. Sturdy vagrants were to be whipped and sent on to the next parish. Genuine cases of distress were to be met with outdoor relief paid from the local rates. Every parish had to support a workhouse for the sick and old who had no-one else to look after them. By the early nineteenth century this system was breaking down. In the recession during and following the Napoleonic wars genuine distress had grown out of all proportion. The Speenhamland system attempted to deal with it by topping up wages in accordance with the fluctuating price of bread. But unscrupulous farmers exploited these well-meant measures by paying below minimum wages and laying off hands altogether during slack seasons, thus throwing their upkeep onto the rates. The price of poor relief soared. Poor rates that had totalled £2 million in 1775 had doubled by 1801 and by 1831 had reached £7 million.

Ignoring the reality that during periods of economic downturn the jobs that the supposedly idle poor were shirking did not even exist, the principle behind the new Poor Law was to make the conditions under which relief could be given so unattractive that the poor would be driven to accept jobs, even at the most pitifully low wages. Outdoor relief was abolished and the old parish workhouses discontinued. In their place parishes were joined together, each union, as it was called, to be served by a new purpose built institution. Even as Darwin stepped off *The Beagle* at Falmouth these grim Malthusian fortresses were arising, red brick and raw at cross roads and on the outskirts of every sizeable town. It was an archipelago of concentration camps. Families were to be split up and the sexes kept rigorously separated. Inmates were to work long hours at the hardest tasks such as stone breaking and picking oakum. The food was to be of the meanest and the most unpalatable. Bells were not even to be tolled at pauper funerals. As always when states impose cruel and unjust laws, there was no lack of sadists coming forward to implement them. Rumours abounded about the miseries of those unfortunates who had had no option but to enter these 'bastilles' as they were popularly known, only outdone by the atrocities that were actually recorded. In the Warwick workhouse a two year old child was punished for dirtying himself by having his own excrement stuffed into his mouth. In the Hoo Union the master was reprimanded for pruriently flogging teenage girls. An inmate was sent to Knutsford gaol for fetching his infant to his own bed when he heard it crying in another part of the workhouse.[11]

The discontent aroused by the new poor law brought even greater social tensions that expressed themselves in the Chartist movement. The Chartists demanded a national charter guaranteeing annual parliaments and a greatly extended voting franchise. In the autumn of 1838 tens of thousands met by night on the Lancashire moors to swear allegiance to the Charter, where, according to R.G. Gammage, the only Chartist to attempt a history of the movement, the banners inscribed with death's heads 'viewed by the red light of the glaring torches, presented a scene of awful grandeur'. At a meeting held on August bank holiday Monday 1839 at Halifax it was reckoned that 200,000 people were present.[12] The spectre of millions on the march and the nation-wide organization of Chartism provoked hysterical levels of anxiety and terror in the authorities and the middle and upper classes they represented.

It was into this maelstrom that the politically inactive Darwin inadvertently plunged when he moved to London in January 1837, staying with his brother Erasmus at his lodgings in Great Marlborough Street. Darwin came to London to have his precious pampas fossils classifed by Richard Owen, the new Hunterian Professor at the Royal College of Surgeons in Lincon's Inn Fields and the great anatomist of the day; to have the pickled birds he had assumed were varieties of finch assessed by the famous ornithologist and taxidermist John Gould at the Royal Zoological Society's museum, where Gould told him to his astonishment that the finches were not varieties but separate species; and to have his views on evolution yet more unsettled by Thomas Bell, Professor of Zoology at King's College in the Strand, who informed him that his giant tortoises were native to the Galapagos. How to explain so idiosyncratic a species in so isolated a place? Erasmus's house was one of the social centres of scientific London. The returned voyager found himself lionized by luminaries who before his epic circumnavigation had been distant and godlike Olympians. Lyell, whose *Principles of Geology* had been Darwin's second Bible during the voyage of *The Beagle,* greatly undermining his confidence in the account of creation given in the first; Babbage, the inventor of the mechanical calculator; Thomas Carlyle; and Darwin's cousin Hensleigh Wedgwood, making a name for himself as a student of the evolution of language; together with most of the scientific movers and shakers in London, all of these were frequent visitors.[13]

The sciences were not the only topics of conversation ardently debated at Erasmus's table. Great Marlborough Street was also a fortress of Malthusian doctrine. Another frequent visitor was Harriet Martineau. Erasmus and she were so close that Fanny Wedgwood, Hensleigh's wife, thought that they might as well be already married, though in fact they never were.. Martineau was famous as the chief proponent of Malthus's views in England. Her fictionalised *Illustrations Of Political Economy,* featuring heroic members of the lower orders who withstood the temptations to sexual intercourse in order to keep population down and improve their station in life, were immensely popular with the middle classes. In fact, Martineau had sent some of her stories out to Darwin while *The Beagle* was visiting South America, exhorting him to distribute them amongst the ship's crew in the hope that the sailors might desist from increasing population while visiting foreign ports, though whether with happy result Darwin did not record. At these scintillating soirees – 'worth all other, & more brilliant kinds, many times over' confided Darwin to his journal – scientific topics were discussed interchangeably with the fiery and volatile politics of the day. Middle class values were taken for granted, Malthusian ideals part of the intellectual fabric. Malthus's reduction of his ideas to mathematical demonstration, his irrefutable argument that the geometrical increase of population was always going to outdistance the sequential production of food, could not be countered. That giving the starving poor food would only enable their children to survive, and by increasing their numbers would only make their starvation worse, was irrefutable. Malthus had science on his side.

Carlyle's hostility to the new poor law only served to burnish the enthusiasm of Erasmus and Harriet Martineau.. The value of unrestricted competition, and the importance of free trade, factory expansion and the removal of religious disabilities were debated endlessly. The principles of politics were being redefined by the latest discoveries of the scientists. The view expressed in a letter to Lyell by the doyen of them all, Sir John Herschel who was still in South Africa but whom Darwin had met at the Cape, a meeting that at the time had seemed far more important than the encounter with the finches on the Galapagos, in which Herschel had referred to the origin of new species as 'the mystery of mysteries', was pored over as if it were holy writ. These evangelical Whigs increasingly saw religion as discredited by higher German Biblical criticism – George Eliot and her unmarried lover G.H. Lewes were also visitors who were especially taken by higher Germans – and by the fossils recorded in Lyell's geology, although Lyell himself clung to the special and separate creation of man by God almost till the end. It was to an ancient world of competition, in which there had been winners and losers, the survivors and the disappeared, that the fossils attested. The second important thing we have to realize about Darwin is how inextricably linked were politics and science, evolution and poor law reform, in the background of his thinking during this most crucial and formative period of his life. At Erasmus's table science and politics were inseparable. The scientific examination of nature was corroborating Whig ideals. '... if society does not want his labour' said Malthus of a workman who cannot find work 'at Nature's mighty feast there is no cover for him. She tells him to be gone and will quickly execute her orders'.

Erasmus' brilliant social circle was not the only point at which evolutionary science and politics crossed. Medicine was also a crucial crossroads of interaction. Robert Darwin had sent Charles to study medicine in Edinburgh because Edinburgh, where he himself had studied, was the leading medical school in the kingdom. With the ending of the Napoleonic wars many Edinburgh students had gone to study in Paris, the hospital and post-mortem facilities there being superior, and cadavers cheap and legal. Among them was Robert Grant, who had become a lecturer on the anatomy of invertebrate animals by the time Darwin arrived in Edinburgh in 1825. Uninterested in medicine and sickened by operations and dissections, Darwin had greatly enjoyed collecting shells with Grant on the Scottish seashores and was greatly influenced by Grant's ferocious materialism and the Lamarckian evolutionary views he had picked up in France.[14] The medical schools of Paris were a hotbed of anatomical and political dissension. On the one hand Georges Cuvier was Professor of Comparative Anatomy and also a counsellor of state. He was an ultra-Royalist who feared the return of revolutionary turmoil and advocated a strong centralized government. He saw his political views validated by his approach to anatomy. Each species was stable and complete in itself, its anatomical form explained purely by the function that each limb or organ was called upon to perform. There were no intermediate forms and any structural similarities between species were fortuitous.

Geoffroi St Hilaire, on the other hand, taught the evolution of Lamarck. Species were fluid, constantly changing and profoundly interconnected. There was no permanent order of nature. The advance of species was to be explained by individuals developing, through their own efforts, features and habits that they hand on to their progeny. Thus, the giraffe that acquires a longer neck through constant straining after the topmost leaves hands on this characteristic to offspring who, in their turn, reach after yet higher leaves and hand on a yet longer neck to their own children. The son of the blacksmith is already born with huge muscles developed by his father's hammering. This doctrine, with its implication that the social order is not permanent and God-given, that nature rewards those who pull themselves up by their own bootstraps and that giraffes who have simply inherited long necks are rightfully displaced by other giraffes who by their own efforts have developed still longer ones, greatly appealed to atheistic artisans and revolutionaries. By the 1830s London, with its burgeoning science, had become the centre of anatomical studies, and many medical students now moved to London, bringing their radical evolutionary and social views with them, headed by none other than Darwin's old mentor Robert Grant.

In London these revolutionary scientific and political ideas fused with a home-grown controversy that had been simmering for some time. In 1817 William Lawrence, drawing on ideas already put into currency by Erasmus Darwin and Joseph Priestley, had given a controversial series of lectures to the Royal College of Surgeons, in which he had argued that the human mind is not a special transcendental faculty radically distinguishing man from the other animals, but simply a complex organization of nervous tissue, in principle no different from the mental faculties found in other organic forms. Lawrence relied heavily on the comparative anatomical structures of different species. The brain is in principle no different from any other organ. There is an observable continuity between human and animal brains. Motions of the will can be explained through the irritability of nervous tissue. Even human emotions like love and sympathy can be explained through their analogues in the behaviour of other species, and even ultimately from the chemical affinities of inorganic matter, from which all life has developed. Needless to say, such views were highly explosive in 1817. Both Lawrence and his opponents were aware that anatomical theories had profound moral, social and political implications. Radicals like Paine and Godwin had based their revolutionary arguments on the premise that there was no basis in nature for a divinely ordained social hierarchy. Anatomically all men were equal. The theory that life depended on 'a subtile and mobile fluid' specially infused into it from above', wrote Lawrence, was 'not only designed to show the nature and operation of the cause, by which vital phenomena are produced, but to add a new sanction to the great principles of morality and religion.....to make us all good and virtuous, to impose a restraint upon vice stronger than Bow Street or the Old Bailey can apply'.

The immanentists who followed Lawrence were countered by the transcendentalists, whose spokesman was John Abernethy. Abernethy argued that the order and power of the organism were not properties emergent from below, but had to be imposed by divine intervention from above. He quoted the great eighteenth century surgeon John Hunter – the eponym in whose memory Richard Owen was appointed first Hunterian Professor – to the effect that there was 'some subtile, mobile, invisible substance, superadded to the evident structure of the muscles, or other forms of vegetable and animal matter'.[15] Politics divided along the same lines as biology. Tories held that the social order could not be changed because it was sanctioned by a nature that was unchanging, stable and God-given. Radicals replied that there was nothing sacrosanct about the political and social injustices all about them, for the very reason that nature was not stable and unchanging but fluid and evolving. 'Once it is admitted that the principles of morality rise not from law, tradition and prescription but from the internal admonitions of every man's conscience', wrote Robert Southey to Lord Liverpool, then 'there is an end to our prosperity and peace; the reign of Atheism is established, and Anarchy, and Rapine and Murder are at our doors!'. The prime originators of anarchy and revolution, said Edmund Burke, are philosophers who destroy 'the docility of the mind'. When the lower orders become convinced that 'all antient institutions are the result of ignorance; and all prescriptive government an usurpation', then the fabric of society would be in grave danger.

* * *

By the twenties and thirties the leading Tory theorist was Coleridge and his avatar in the anatomical laboratories Richard Owen. In Coleridgean circles Lawrence's materialism and impiety were tantamount to treason, though having already been acquitted of blasphemous libel in 1817, when, in 1828, he again faced a Chancery case, Lawrence recanted many of his views in order to protect his teaching post. Influenced by German *Naturphilosophie[16]*, Coleridge would have no truck with reductionist and atomistic explanations of living forms. In his view the component parts of an organism were marshalled into order by transcendental organic archetypes, and evolution was to be explained by the increasing clarification of these archetypes and their growing power to organize matter. There was a direct connection between this anatomical archetypal order and the archetype of order underlying society. Harmonious class relations depended on sound scientific foundations, which made eradication of any Lamarckian tendency towards self-development in anatomy essential. For Coleridgean conservatives, one and the same Logos penetrated both nature and society, establishing authority and order in society, church and the natural world. There is 'one Universal Presence' wrote Coleridge, uniting the community of nature with the community of persons.[17] Radical demands for democracy, disestablishment, universal suffrage, popular education, corporation takeover, land taxes and the abolition of church tithes were not only politically inflammatory but abuses of nature.

Of these conservative views Owen was the scientific champion. He found evidence for Coleridge's archetypes in similar anatomical patterns occurring in different species that he called homologies, a repetitive order, according to him, that could only be explained by divine imprint. On the other hand, the gaps between species, especially between man and any other, were anatomically unbridgeable. In a paper in 1835 he showed that the chimpanzee was not a half-way house between ape and man, as Lamarck had claimed, but that its sloping face, protruding snout and 'bestial physiognomy' placed it firmly on the ape side of the impassable abyss between the rest of the mammals and mankind. He proved that the orang could not have been an upright-standing ancestor of the human. The flexor muscle, terminating in a single tendon in the big toe of man, divides into three tendons in the orang, which would prevent it from standing upright but would enable it to grasp the branches of trees. He then went head to head with Grant in a controversy about the so-called Stonesfield 'opossum' fossil.[18] Unearthed at a slate quarry in Oxfordshire, the fossil had what could be interpreted as both reptilian and mammalian characteristics. But, all were agreed, it was also so old that if it were mammalian it would upset the

Lamarckian calendar of evolutionary progress. Grant was therefore out to prove it was a reptile, Owen that it was a mammal, and that the mammalian order had therefore evolved as an independent phylum from the beginning of life.[19]

Owen certainly proved his point to the satisfaction of his fellow Coleridgeans. In his Hunterian lectures to the Royal College of Surgeons in 1837 Owen set out to demonstrate the Ideas and Archetypes underlying different organic forms. He attacked the transformationist idea that in the womb the embryo recapitulates more primitive forms of life, thus testifying to previous organisms from which its own species had developed. He repudiated supposed links between the anatomies of different species: the relation of a lobster's shell rings to vertebrae, the supposed continuum between invertebrates and fish, the link between the gills of a fish and the mammal's inner ear structure. The gaps in the fossil record were so great there was no evidence of the transformationist links the Lamarckians sought. On the other hand, as in the Stonesfield opossum, archetypal formal structures characteristic of mammals, and only mammals, could be seen from the earliest fossil evidence.

The conservative transcendentalists were as politically overt and engaged as the Lamarckian transformationists. To counter the bestialization of man practically as well as theoretically, in 1834 Owen himself enlisted in the Honourable Artillery Company, a vigilante body of merchants and gentry raised to assist the police in putting down working class and chartist demonstrations. On the other side, Thomas Wakley founded *The Lancet* for the specific purpose of linking medical studies with radical politics. The Court of Chancery condemned Lawrence's *Lectures On Man* as blasphemous, which destroyed its copyright. As a result it became a heroic text, to be found on every political dissident's bookshelf. The Chartists were marching under banners that proclaimed with the psalmist 'Dwell in the land and verily thou shalt be fed'. Chartist speeches reviling 'the cruel and detestable doctrines of Malthus' were heard by tens of thousands and reported in *The Times.* Grant was as active a political radical as he was scientifically unorthodox. In the febrile atmosphere, the mainstream London scientists, definitely on the priviliged side of the social divide, saw it as important to discredit Grant's Lamarckism, with its threat to established order, as did Owen.

* * *

The feted Darwin, now secretary of the prestigious Geological Society - a post he had only accepted with the greatest reluctance as a result of Lyell's insistence - watched helpless from his secretary's chair as his old mentor, with many of whose views he secretly sympathized, was invited to speak to the Society on the topic of the Stonesfield opossum, and then, with devastating academic politeness, taken apart limb from limb. Darwin learned from the episode how important it was to keep unorthodox evolutionary views hidden. In Lamarck the radicals had an anatomical justification for their politics. In Owen the Tories had one for theirs. In the three cornered struggle for the land of England, only the Whigs, still dependent on Malthus for philosophical validation, lacked a grounding in evolutionary, or on the conservative side non-evolutionary, biology. Their need was urgent. Neither, on the one hand, able to call upon radical evolutionary doctrine, for Lamarck had been appropriated by the political radicals, nor, on the other, upon divine pattern, for it was the Tory order that was ecclesiastically approved, only the most rigorous science could justify the inhumane treatment they were meting out to their fellow beings. Darwin, nursing his ideas in secret, could not but have been influenced by these events.

(Endnotes)

1   Moore and Desmond in their *Darwin* 1992 London Penguin
    make a convincing case for the importance of Darwin's
    Whig upbringing in the genesis of his idea

2   Helmshore Hist Soc

3   quoted in Chris Aspin new ed. 2007 *The First Industrial
    Society:A Social History of Lancashre 1750-1850*
    Carnegie Press Lancaster UK p.54

4   Helmshore Hist .Soc. .

5   quoted in Aspin *op.cit*

6   Friedrich Engels 1844 *The Condition of theWorking Class
    in England.* Oxford World Classics 1999 .

7   J.F.C. Harrison 1988. *Early Victorian Britain 1832- 51.*
    p. 37. London Fontana

8   Harrison *op. cit.* p. 74

9   Helmshore Hist Soc

10 Harrison *op. cit.* p. 36

11 Harrison p. 88

12 Harrison pp.155-156

13 Desmond and More *Darwin* 1992 London Penguin . ch. 14

14 Janet Browne *Charles Darwin: Vol 1 Voyaging* 2003
    Jonathan Cape ch. 3

15 L. Jacyna : Immanence or Transcendence?: Theories of Life
    and Organization in Britain 1790-1835, *ISIS* 1983 74: 311-329

16 *Naturphilosophie* was a largely German
    phenomenon originating with Schelling and adopted
    by Goethe. It held that material organic forms were
    to be explained by immaterial archetypes underlying them.

17 Adrian Desmond 1989 *The Politics of Evolution.*
    pp. 265. Chicago. Univ of Chicago Press

18 M. Grene and D. Depew 2004 *The Philosophy of Biology:
    An Episodic History.* Cambridge CUP. P.183

19 Desmond and Moore *op. cit.* 275-291

Chapter 4
Darwin: The Intellectual Background

'In October 1838, that is, fifteen months after I had begun my systematic enquiry, I happened to read for amusement Malthus's essay *On Population,* and being well prepared to appreciate the struggle for existence which everywhere goes on from long-continued observation of the habits of animals and plants, it at once struck me that under these circumstances favourable variations would tend to be preserved, and unfavourable ones to be destroyed. The result of this would be the formation of new species. I had at last got a theory by which to work...' Thus Charles Darwin described his great moment of insight many years later in his *Autobiography.*[1] He writes, curiously, as if he had previously never heard of Malthus, and had only come across his work as one might pick up an intriguing title in a second-hand bookshop. In fact he must have heard about Malthus's ideas morning, noon and night at Erasmus's table. How strange too that he read 'for amusement' the text that was at the centre of the searing controversies that were cleaving England. He also gives the impression that his mind was prepared to grasp the significance of Malthus's struggle for existence only by a most purely Baconian collection of data, quite unstained by any philosophical, political or social colouring. In fact this was not the case. Darwin understood the data before him in the way he did, because of the mind he had and the way it had been shaped at Shrewsbury, Edinburgh, Cambridge, on *The Beagle,* and finally in London. We know what he read during his course at Cambridge, and who influenced him, and, from his notebooks, the texts he was reading during the period leading up to October 1838.

* * *

It is crucially important in understanding Darwin and why he interpreted his material as erroneously as he did, to appreciate that, apart perhaps from Lyell's *Principles of Geology,* not only Malthus himself but most of these influences were either misleading or wrong. What were these unfortunate influences?

114

1. Locke's *Essay Concerning Human Understanding.*

At Cambridge Darwin followed a general degree preparatory to gaining a further qualification in divinity, which in fact he never attempted because, instead of returning to Cambridge, he accepted the invitation to join Captain Fitzroy on *The Beagle.* The course was a general one, largely comprised of moral philosophy, some classics, mathematics and what was called natural philosophy, not quite science in our understanding of the term but more a study of the mathematical properties of Newtonian physics. There were only two set books, Locke's *Essay Concerning Human Understanding* and William Paley's *A View of the Evidences Of Christianity,* but these the student was expected to know more or less by heart. Locke was thought to be of particular importance, because his philosophical ideas underpinned the scientific advances of the seventeenth century that had culminated in Newton. It was Locke and Bacon, together with Herschel and Whewell whose influences we will examine later, who shaped Darwin's whole understanding of what science was. The philosophical framework within which he approached the evidence of the finches and the Galapagos turtles was that of Locke's epistemology.

Darwin's thinking is thoroughly in tune with Locke's two fundamental axioms: we gain all our knowledge through our senses, and only our knowledge of primary qualities, not secondary, can give us a direct account of what is happening in the world. Darwin's patient acquisition of factual details that he had seen with his own eyes, or heard with his own ears from animal and plant breeders, was thoroughly Lockean. For Locke the mind is a *tabula rasa.* There are no universal principles already innate in the mind. Otherwise, he argues, children and idiots would be familiar with the law of contradiction, which patently they are not. Reason is the faculty whereby we deduce unknown truths from known ones. If there were innate known principles there would therefore have to be even prior innate known ones from which we had deduced them, which is patently absurd. On the contrary, it is by actually looking at things that we come to know what is true and learn to distinguish real facts from Aristotelian and scholastic gobbledygook. '...we should make greater progress in the discovery of rational and contemplative knowledge if we sought it in the fountain, in the consideration of things themselves...'[2]. What you have to do is to actually look at what is out there, '...all our knowledge of corporeal things lies in our senses'[3].

Yet wait. This is indeed true, he says, but only in a sense. It is perhaps paradoxical, but taking a look is, at first, precisely what doesn't give us truth. It only gives us knowledge of secondary qualities such as sweet and warm and coloured that do not lie in things themselves but in our senses. What we have to do is to bypass what is only in our senses and get at the primary qualities that are in the things themselves: solidity, extension, figure and mobility. 'From whence I think it is easy to draw this observation. That the idea of primary qualities of bodies, are resemblances of them, and their patterns do really exist in the bodies themselves; but the ideas, produced in us by these secondary qualities, have no resemblance of them at all'[4]. The problem is that we never see things as purely extended or moving but always as something which is coloured and sweet or warm *as well as* extended and moving. The great advance of science is to have found a way of seeing things as simply extended and moving with the "white noise" of colour and sweetness cut out. This is why, at last, the experimental methods of seventeenth century science are leading men to what is really true. Directly before us there is a sweet and warm and coloured world that appears to be true because it is so immediately and sensibly there. But actually it isn't the true world.

117

Behind it there is an immediately invisible but mentally knowable world that is the really true one.

* * *

Myth has been replaced by science. This is the mental framework that Locke bequeathed to Darwin. It is crucially important in understanding Darwin's approach. It is from sense experience that we first learn facts, the patient accumulation of observations about turtles, finches, worms and barnacles. But the facts so observed are not the real truth, for they are filtered to us through our sense experiences. What we have to do is to go behind this deceptively sensed world to the really true world of mathematical law. This is exactly how Darwin approached living organisms in *The Origin Of Species.* The world of living nature may appear at first sight to be sweet and harmonious, as Paley thought it was. But the appearance is deceptive. Behind it, for Darwin, there is a real world of strife and competition and incessant war. Nor did Darwin think, as he is often taken as doing, that this was a matter of chance. On the contrary, the struggle for survival was an implacable law that belonged to the inner abstract world, the true world known only to science.

Locke was wrong. It is simply not the case that there is a relatively unreal world known immediately by our senses which is only an indirect reflection of a true world behind it which is known only to science. Our knowledge of Locke's primary qualities does not have a privileged truth status. It is in fact as subjective as our knowledge of secondary ones. If we had a different set of senses than those that evolution has provided us with, then we would see the world very differently. If our senses were refined enough we would, perhaps, not see tables as solid extended objects but as mostly empty spaces defined by positionally indefinable energy events. Would we then be seeing the world as it truly is? It is the condition towards which we are reaching when we extend the scope of our senses by using microscopes and telescopes. But however much this new way of seeing the world might enable us to make hitherto unthinkable deductions about it, the fact would remain that the deductions took as their point of departure new acts of sense that were no more privileged than the familiar old ones. They would just be different. A race of beings whose natural sense faculties were not eyes and ears but microscopes and telescopes would, most likely, praise not the reductive but the inflative method of science.

Such beings would doubtless find a way of viewing a table not in the boring familiar way that *another* set of beings could only guess at by building cyclotrons, but by building laboratories that reproduced conditions in drawing rooms in Kensington. Amazing! It looked *solid.* Now that's what I call *real.* There must be a *really real* world in which matter is not composed mostly of empty space but is continually contiguous. It's the supposedly real-behind-the-imagined but in fact still imaginary picture, or so we imagine, that we always take as holding primary truth.

The defect of the secondary qualities that we naively assume to inhere in things, is, according to Locke, that they disappear when analysed. Whereas primary qualities are 'utterly inseparable from the body, in what state soever it be'[5]. '...take a grain of wheat, divide it into two parts, each part still has solidity, extension, figure and mobility; divide it again, and it retains still the same qualities: and so divide it on, till the parts become insensible, they must retain still each of them all those same qualities'[6]. When they are broken down, colour and sweetness dissolve into another set of categories, whereas the primary qualities do not. But this is exactly what a more recent physics has shown not to be the case. Solid tables are shown not to be composed of contiguous billiard ball atoms, smaller granted, but as solid and figured and mobile as the tables are. Absolutely not. Solidity and extension dissolve into a different thought world defined by a wholly revolutionary set of intellectual co-ordinates, as conceptually far removed from solidity as experienced red is from vibrating light waves. There is another dimension of reality behind extension, one that has now been discovered by quantum physics, just as there was another dimension of reality behind colour. Doubtless, the history of science might well suggest, there will turn out to be another dimension behind quantum and, for all we know, yet another dimension behind that. Far from these dimensions being ever more unmythical and verifiably the ground of empirical truth, it turns out, as quantum so graphically attests, that they so defy reason and common sense as only to be approachable through myths even more imaginary than the everyday world, the one known through Locke's deluding secondary sense perceptions, with which we started.

This is a basic mistake that Locke made and handed on to Darwin. Extension and motion, or Einsteinian relativity, or quantum physics, are no more truly real than the world in which we get up in the morning, go to work and have lunch. They are just different aspects of a single reality. It is a mistake that permeates the whole of *The Origin Of Species.* In fact, animals are behaving in no more real or true a way when they are killing each other or getting to scarce food sources before other animals, than they are when they are sleeping, sunning themselves or building dens and nests.

2. Paley's *Natural Theology.*

It is often thought that Darwin simply overthrew Paley. Paley's designed world was replaced by Darwin's undesigned one. But this is a gross over-simplification. Darwin was so influenced by Paley that he never escaped from him. He came to the opposite conclusion to Paley only in so far as he never ceased to move within Paley's thought world, even to the end. He was absolutely steeped in Paley's approach. As an undergraduate he lived in the very same rooms in the first court of Christ's that Paley himself had inhabited thirty years before. Forced by university statute to read

Paley's *Evidences,* he was so impressed by it he went on to read the *Natural Theology* purely out of personal choice, paying rapt attention to every word, he tells us in his *Autobiography.* The opening paragraph of the *Natural Theology* was one of the best known passages in the whole of the literature of England:

'If in crossing a heath, suppose I pitched my foot against a *stone,* and were asked how the stone came to be there, I might possibly answer that, for any thing I knew to the contrary, it had lain there for ever: nor would it perhaps be very easy to shew the absurdity of this answer. But suppose I had found a *watch* upon the ground, and it should be enquired how the watch happened to be in that place. I should hardly think of the answer I had before given, that, for anything I knew, the watch might always have been there. Yet why should not this answer serve for the watch as well as for the stone? Why is it not as admissable in the second case, as in the first? For this reason, and for no other, viz. that, when we come to inspect the watch, we perceive (what we could not discover in the stone) that its several parts are framed and put together for a purpose... the inference, we think, is inevitable; that the watch must have had a maker; that there must have existed, at some time or some place or other, an artificer or artificers who formed it for the purpose which we find it actually to answer; who comprehended its construction and designed its use'.[7]

It is not without significance that Paley was the son of a clock maker. It is also often thought that his is the classic statement of the argument from design. In fact this is not the case. The emphasis in the really classic statements, such as that of Thomas Aquinas in his fifth argument for the existence of God in the *Summa Theologiae,* is on the paradox of apparently intelligent behaviour in things and creatures that lack intelligence. The arrow shot by an archer seeks an end. But only intelligent creatures can act for an end. In seeking its end, therefore, the arrow must be guided by an intelligence that is not its own. Aquinas's argument does not exclude the possibility that the construction of a thing, even a living creature, might have come about by purely natural means. He is solely concerned to solve the paradox of how an unintelligent thing or creature can act purposefully. Nor does Aquinas argue, or even imply, that the entity 'all men call God' is without rather than within the universe. In fact he does the opposite. He was operating in a context where, in the University of Paris, people were accusing him of atheism because he had adopted Aristotle's ideas, and Aristotle's first cause was not without but within the universe. He was not, in fact, trying to prove the existence of God at all in our sense. The word he uses is 'probare', which doesn't mean to logically demonstrate but to test, as, in a case where we still preserve this original sense, we might prove silver. What he was doing, in this sense of testing, was proving Aristotle's ideas, and showing that they are not incompatible with a Christian belief in God. He goes on in Quaestio 8 of *Prima Pars,* in fact, to devote a whole question to the immanence of God in the universe.

Paley's version of the design argument is completely different. He was writing for a machine age. Aquinas's approach is by no means incompatible with Darwin's - or rather, as I shall argue in the next chapter, Darwin would never have interpreted his data in the way he did if he had been thinking like Aquinas rather than Paley – whereas Paley's is. Paley's emphasis was on the intricacy and perfection of the natural machines we see all around us, particularly the living ones, so beautifully constructed that they must have had a constructor. But in treating organisms as machines rather than souls Paley had already unwittingly opened the way to Darwin's materialism. There is no way in which the constructor of a machine is part of the machine that he constructs. He is by definition extrinsic to it. Once Darwin was able to show that it was possible for the intricate construction of organisms to have come about by natural means, the case for the extrinsic constructor completely collapsed. Because not only Darwin but almost everybody else in Victorian England was so influenced by Paley, Darwin was able to avoid the issue of whether talking about organisms as if they were natural machines is an appropriate way to talk about organisms. Perhaps it is. But Darwin was able to get away without even raising the question.

Paley does not appeal to scenic grandeur or hierarchical orders of being, as proponents of the argument from design had traditionally done, but to ingenious contrivance. Although he does discuss chemistry and astronomy, his argument rests overwhelmingly on anatomy, and extremely precise and closely observed anatomical examples. He does not attempt to persuade by logic but by weight of instances. How can we explain such ingenuities of contrivance in the natural world we see about us, and above all in our own bodies, except by reference to the most ingenious of contrivers? Far from appealing to the beauty or sublimity of the natural world, his argument is that nature's contrivances are artificial, the consequence of artifice, more artificial indeed than any man-made machine could ever be. 'Muscles, with their tendons, are the instruments with which animal motion is performed. It will be our business to point out instances in which, and properties with respect to which, the disposition of these muscles is as strictly mechanical, as that of the wires and strings of a puppet.[8]' 'I challenge any man to produce, in the joints and pivots of the most complicated, or the most flexible machine, that was ever contrived, a construction more artificial, or more evidently artificial, than that which is seen in the vertebrae of the *human neck.*[9] 'Observe a new-born child opening its eyelids. What does the opening of the curtain discover? The anterior part of two pellucid globes, which, when they come to be examined, are found to be constructed upon strict optical principles; the self-same principles upon which we ourselves construct optical instruments.'[10]

Because they are such beautiful machines, the

different parts of these perfect contrivances are perfectly adapted to their purpose. 'It were, however, injustice to dismiss the eyes as a piece of mechanism, without noticing that most exquisite of all contrivances, the nictitating membrane, which is found in the eyes of birds and of many quadrupeds. Its use is to sweep the eye, which it does in an instant; to spread over in the lachrymose humor; to defend it also from sudden injuries; yet not totally, when withdrawn upon the pupil, to shut out the light.'[11] 'The ear, it is probable, is no less artificially and mechanically adapted to its office than is the eye.'[12] The body, to use Paley's own quaint word, is beautifully packaged. 'Observe the heart pumping at the centre, at the rate of eighty strokes a minute; one set of pipes carrying the stream away from it; another set, bringing, in its course, the fluid back to it again; the lungs performing their elaborate office viz. distending and contracting their many thousand vesicles, by a reciprocation that cannot cease for a minute: the stomach exercising its perfect chymistry; the bowels silently propelling the changed aliment; collecting from it, as it proceeds, and transmitting to the blood an incessant supply of prepared and assimilated nourishment; the blood pursuing its course; the liver, the kidneys, the pancreas, the parotid, with many other known and distinguishable glands, drawing off from it, all the while, their proper secretions.'[13] Yet all these different organs are operating within a body that is perfectly symmetrical. They are so cleverly "packaged" that no matter how violently a tumbler or a dancer flings his body about, they continue to enact their ministrations in perfect harmony and order.

The creator is not only ingenious but also good. His goodness rests, according to Paley, upon two observations. The design of the contrivances he has made is beneficial to them. And, secondly, 'the Deity has superadded *pleasure* to animal sensations beyond what was necessary for any other purpose, or when the purpose, so far as it is necessary, might have been achieved by the operation of pain'[14]. It is true that there is pain in the world. But even pain is beneficial. If animals did not feel pain they would not know to avoid that which was harmful to them. Death is necessary, for without death there could be no life, and even the pains of death have been much mitigated by the author of life. 'Brutes are largely delivered from anxiety on this account by reason of the inferiority of their faculties' and even in man, and here Paley surely speaks as the country rector who had attended many a death bed, when death comes at the end of a long illness it does not hold the terrors ascribed to it by those in a state of health.

* * *

Paley even answers Malthus. It is true that the geometric increase of population will always over take provision, for the 'increase of provision, even under the circumstances the most advantageous, can only assume the form of an arithmetic series'[15]. But even Malthus is part of a beneficent plan. For if human beings were allowed to breed indiscriminately they would marry so early as to overtake all provision and would be able to obtain it without that 'toilsome endeavour' which is good for the soul. 'It is a happy world after all. The air, the earth, the water teem with delighted existence. In a spring noon, or on a summer evening, on which ever side I turn my eyes myriads of happy beings crowd upon my view....... Swarms of new born *flies* are trying their pinions upon the air. Their sportive motions, their wanton mazes, their gratuitous activity, their continued change of place without want or purpose, testify their joy, and the exhilaration they feel in their lately discovered faculties. A *bee* among the flowers in spring, is one of the cheerfullest objects that can be looked upon. Its life appears to be all enjoyment, so busy and so pleased...'[16]

The trouble was that Darwin had looked at organic creatures even more closely than Paley, and whereas Paley was delighted, the exquisitely sensitive and compassionate Darwin was appalled. Where Paley saw flies dancing for joy, Darwin saw the larva of the ichneumon fly eating away from the inside the body of the live caterpillar in which it had been laid by its parent. Overwhelmed by the horror of the nature he had studied so minutely, Darwin had no option but to reject Paley, whose whole argument was that nature is artificially contrived and not horrific but benign. If Darwin had had theological resources other than Paley he might have understood descent with modification very differently.

3. Herschel and Whewell

The Cambridge to which Darwin went up in 1828 was small and intimate. By today's standards it was astonishingly amateurish.[17] Darwin's greatest mentor, the Revd J.S. Henslow who recommended him for *The Beagle,* had been Professor of Mineralogy before he took over the completely moribund faculty of Botany. The Reverend Adam Sedgwick likewise knew no Geology when he became Woodwardian Professor in that subject, a post he campaigned for on the slogan that at least he knew nothing, whereas what his opponent knew was all wrong. Charles Babbage, Lucasian Professor of Mathematics while Darwin was at Cambridge, the illustrious seat once occupied by Newton and now by Stephen Hawking, declined to give any lectures at all. William Whewell, who became Master of Trinity in 1842, was a specialist in nothing who acted as if he knew everything. But these great and highly intelligent men, learning as they went, had an enthusiasm for their subjects and a capacious grasp of them that totally enthralled the undergraduate Darwin, whose intimate relationship with his teachers would be impossible today. Babbage invented the mathematical calculator. Henslow was the finest botanist in England. Sedgwick, together with Lyell, became the greatest geologist in the world. Whewell bestrode the intellectual firmament as no-one else was to do until Jowett at Balliol fifty years later. Henslow's scientific evenings, followed by Darwin's walks back to college afterwards with Whewell – 'after Sir J. Mackintosh the best discourser on grave subjects I ever heard' - and the long vacation Darwin spent with Sedgwick studying geology in Wales - Sedgwick discovering the Cambrian system and creating modern geology as they proceeded - was as scintillating and stimulating an education as anyone could possibly have had.[18]

It is not surprising therefore that Darwin deeply imbibed these mens' passionate beliefs in what science was. Their philosophy had been articulated most magisterially by Sir John Herschel in his *Preliminary Discourses on the Study of Natural Philosophy,* that Darwin read during his last year at Cambridge in 1831, and later in 1840 by Whewell himself in *The Philosophy of the Inductive Sciences.* According to this view, science first proceeds by collecting data in a manner as unprejudiced by any theoretical ideas as possible. But the data are then subject to rigorous reasoning, first inductive and then deductive, to discover the laws underlying them. These laws are of two kinds. At a more superficial level there are empirical laws that describe the regularities to be observed in phenomena. These are the ones discoverable by induction. Kepler's discovery of the orbits of the planets would be an example of them. But underlying these there are still more fundamental laws, what Herschel called *verae causae,* that explain causally why the regularities occur. Newton's laws of motion are supreme examples of such *verae causae.*

These causal laws are abstract and universal. They can only be discovered by deductive reasoning. They do not describe how things happen to be but how they must be. The acid test of their validity is when they lead to observations not yet made, often in surprising quarters which otherwise would never have been examined, that confirm their truth, what Whewell called the consilience of inductions. This is exactly the procedure Darwin follows in *The Origin.* First of all he collects data on variations, in the first instance from plant and animal breeders. Then he observes the same data in nature. Then he deduces an empirical law based on these observations: all animals breed up to and beyond the holding capacity of their environment, even so slow a breeder as the elephant that produces only three pairs of young during its breeding life of thirty to ninety years. Deduction remorselessly indicates that from one single pair, fifteen million elephants would have descended within five hundred years. [19] He then deduces that there *must,* therefore, be a struggle for existence, and as a further logical entailment that there *must* be natural selection. This was a method that had worked spendidly for Newtonian astronomy. It was fatally misleading when applied to living organisms.

4. Comte and Quetelet.

In August 1838 Darwin read Sir David Brewster's review of Comte's *Cours de Philosophie Positive* in the Edinburgh Review.[20] His notebooks record that it had a profound impact on him. Brewster presents Comte's view that

> 'all real science stands in radical and necessary opposition to all theology; and this character is more strongly indicated in astronomy than in any other... No science has given such terrible blows to the doctrine of final causes... the indispensable basis of all religious systems.'

Comte's thesis was that everything that had once been explained by theological mystery can, and ultimately will be, explained by rationally apprehensible natural law. Astronomy, chemistry, physics and physiology have already been reduced to positive theories. In time what Comte calls 'social physics' will also be explicable without any recourse to the divine. Comte outlines the principles of a positive philosophy that might guide those who are venturing into these less physical and more social fields. The purpose of all science is to discover general laws that will permit prediction. It is characteristic of science to discover that those things that had appeared to be isolated and chance phenomena are, in fact, regularities explicable by law. Darwin was especially struck by Comte's treatment of the eccentricities of the solar system. In his Bridgewater Treatise that Darwin had read in 1838 (the Duke of Bridgewater had left a bequest financing a series of annual lectures to demonstrate the existence of God) Whewell had argued that there are accidental features of the solar system – the distance of the planets from the sun, the inclination of their orbits, their periods of rotation – that cannot be accounted for by Newton's laws. Yet these are essential for human life, and therefore examples of God's providence. Comte showed, to Darwin's satisfaction, that these features of the solar system were not accidental at all but could all be accounted for by law.

His growing belief that chance and accident are not in fact accidental was further confirmed when he read a review a month later, in *The Athenaeum,* of Quetelet's *Sur l'homme.*[21] Quetelet's book was an examination of what was known about statistical laws, which were becoming vitally important for the insurance companies and the speculations in financial futures underpinning the burgeoning industrial revolution. A single accident viewed as an isolated case we view as uncaused and happening by chance. But the greater the number of similar accidents we examine the more we find we can predict general regularities, even though each isolated instance remains as impervious to rational explanation as ever it was. Given known numbers of a statistical population, underwriters and actuaries can predict the exact number of railway accidents that will occur, or the exact number of deaths from tuberculosis, to an astonishing degree. What this shows is that isolated accidents are not ruled by chance at all. When they are enumerated and examined generally the general laws that rule them begin to show through. The more universal the population, the more universally absolute – the closer to a *vera causa* in fact – the law. Quetelet was a follower of Laplace. Accidents only appear to be accidental because we do not know enough about their causes. If we knew enough about the laws underlying phenomena we could predict certainly which way a particular throw of the dice would fall, or whether there would be an accident on a particular railway journey, in every instance. There is room in the world neither for God nor chance. Darwin was immensely impressed.

In fact he was grievously misled. Now we know more about the laws that actually do underly phenomena we have found the exact opposite. The more fundamental you go down the more events are ruled not by certainty but by radical uncertainty.

5. Dugal Stewart on Adam Smith

Another work that greatly influenced Darwin in the crucial weeks leading up to the insight of October 1838 was Dugal Stewart's *Biographical Memoir of Adam Smith.*[22]

It was from this that he derived the important idea that social phenomena can only be understood from the actions of individual agents, and that if individuals are left to themselves to pursue their own interests a stable and evolving society will automatically emerge, without the intervention of a designing and directing mind.[23] The analogies between (1) the individual economic agent and individual variation as the unit of selection, and (2) a dynamic economic ordering automatically producing itself without government interference and the biological ordering produced automatically by natural selection, without Paley's divine contriver, are obvious. Darwin, however, had little idea of the circumstances under which Stewart's *Memoir* had been written. Adam Smith died in 1790. By 1792 Scotland was gripped by anti-French hysteria and was thought to be on the brink of revolution.[24] Against this background, Smith's French ideas were thought to have inspired popular argumentation, discontent, anti-war sentiments and opposition to the English government. The hero of 'the liberal young of Edinburgh'[25], Smith was viewed with the deepest suspicion by more conservative factions.

Adam Smith was before all else a man of the enlightenment. As with Kant, his central belief was that man's possession of a transcendental intellect lifts both his reason and his feelings above the local and the immediate onto a universal plane. He was not, most importantly, an economist in the modern sense, but Professor of Ethics and Jurisprudence at Glasgow University. He gave an annual course of lectures that was divided into four parts. After the first, each subsequent part was built upon the ideas that had been established by its predecessors. The first division of the lectures was concerned with what his age called natural philosophy, but we would call physics and cosmology, and was published under the title *A History of Astronomy*. The second was about the foundational principles of ethical behaviour, and was published under the title *The Theory of Moral Sentiments*. The third part was about prudence, i.e. the art of putting ethical principles into practice in actual life and was published under the title *The Wealth of Nations*. The fourth part was about jurisprudence and was never published, but notes taken from Smith's lectures were discovered in a country house at the end of the nineteenth century, so we have some idea of what this part of the course contained. So we see that *The Wealth of Nations* is not primarily about how to get rich but about how to be good. It is about putting into action the principles laid down in *The Theory of Moral Sentiments*.

* * *

Smith's big ethical idea is sympathy. But he doesn't mean by it, as Darwin presumed, feeling sorry for somebody. What he means is the ability that humans have to imagine themselves in somebody else's shoes. We demand justice, he says, not because of some abstract principle but because we *imagine* the outrage on somebody else's behalf that we would feel if the injustice were being done to us. He agrees that we are naturally selfish. But in *living life* we learn not to be. Suppose I prick my thumb, he says. To me it is the worst pain in the world. But it is obvious to *the bystanders,* much as they might feel sorry for me, that the suffering of people starving to death in China is worse.[26] Because it is natural to me to please my fellows and to be influenced by them, gradually their point of view moderates my own. I too come to see that the suffering of starving Chinese is worse, until in the end the bystanders' point of view also becomes mine. When I was a small child, he says, it was obvious to me that my thumb was bigger than a mountain. But as I grow up I learn about perspective, and when I am an adult *it never even occurs to me that my thumb might be bigger.* I start off naturally selfish but through social intercourse I become naturally unselfish. It is by our intercourse with each other that we learn to be unselfish moral beings. We develop what he calls 'the man within the breast'. We absorb each others' moral being into our own. And we do this not by attending ethics lectures but in the comings and goings of ordinary life. This is why he is so keen on dismantling trade barriers. Through commerce we *absorb other peoples' being* into ourselves and become not just financially richer but, far more importantly, humanly richer. If we trade with the French instead of putting up customs barriers, not only will they become economically better off by selling us their onions, so that they have more money with which to buy our pottery so that we'll be richer too; we shall have been immensely enriched as people by absorbing all that French sophistication and art of living into ourselves. Smith meant exactly the opposite of the version of his ideas that grew up in the nineteenth century, in Darwin's era, and has continued to dominate most economic thinking ever since: if everybody is encouraged to act entirely selfishly, then in some miraculous way society as a whole will get richer too.

* * *

In the Scottish sedition trials of 1793 Smith's works were a constant point at issue. Thomas Muir, a lawyer, was sentenced to fourteen years transportation for the crime of 'exciting disaffection to government'. In another trial a Unitarian clergyman, Thomas Palmer, quoted Smith as defending the right of even the poorest beggar to discuss reform. But in the eyes of the judge this constituted precise evidence of guilt, and he too was transported. Stewart himself was forced by two Scottish law lords into a recantation of 'every word you have ever uttered, in favour of doctrines which had led to so great a mischief'. Stewart's defence was that he was only talking about economics, not the views of 'the French philosophers'. The radically different ways in which Smith's writings could be interpreted came out during an episode in 1795, in which Samuel Whitbread tried to bring a bill into parliament giving magistrates power to impose a minimum wage. Whitbread quoted Smith arguing for high wages on grounds of equity. 'No society can surely be flourishing and happy, of which the greater part of the members are poor and miserable. It is but equity beside that they who feed, clothe and lodge the whole body... should themselves be tolerably well fed, clothed and lodged'. Pitt responded by quoting back at him the principles of unrestricted free trade laid down by 'the most celebrated writers upon political economy'.[27]

It is hardly surprising that in these circumstances Dugal Stewart in his *Memoir,* written at the very height of the Scottish sedition trials, should give a very restricted version of Adam Smith's doctrines. 'I shall content myself therefore with remarking in the most general terms… to maintain that order of things that nature has pointed out; by allowing *every man,* as long as he observes the rules of justice, to pursue *his own interest* in his own way, and to bring both his interest and his capital into the freest competition with those of his fellow citizens…' Stewart distorted Adam Smith's ideas by making it sound as if he had written about economics in a vacuum, a misconception that was easy to foster since *The Wealth Of Nations* makes so little direct reference to *The Theory Of Moral Sentiments* and the lectures on the supreme importance of justice, in which, in fact, it is so deeply rooted. There is no emphasis in Stewart's *Memoir* on Smith's understanding of the imaginative sympathy of human beings for each other as the basis of economic life, on the importance of universal education so that 'even the meanest beggar' might question the institutions of society, on the supreme importance of state imposed justice as the condition of free trade 'for wherever tradesmen are gathered together they conspire to cheat the public', or on Smith's view that wages should be regulated not simply by supply and demand but also by 'common humanity', and that high wages are the condition of a healthy economy.

Through Dugal Stewart, Darwin took from Adam Smith the very opposite of what the father of economics meant. Smith's whole scheme depends on imaginative sympathy, as he understands that term, between economic agents. The kind of social ordering he advocates is essentially something that can only be brought about by self-conscious participants whose moral consciousness has been formed by those about them. These are exactly the conditions that do not apply amongst animals. The dynamic balance of society is not brought about by a purely automatic mechanism, but by inter-active intelligences. Given that the same kind of natural order resulting from self-interested inter-acting individuals can be observed in animal societies as well as human ones, what Darwin would better have taken from Adam Smith was the same argument, analogously, as that put forward by Aquinas when he discusses action towards an end. Since such phenomena are meaningless without the intervention of intelligence, and non-human creatures do not have that kind of intelligence, then they must be directed by another intelligence, which is not their own. Adam Smith's works, if they had been better understood, might well – even should - have directed Darwin towards, not away from, a divine designer.

6. Malthus

The most damaging and misleading influence by far on Darwin was Malthus himself. By an irony, in adapting what he supposed were Malthusian truths about human populations to animals, Darwin unwittingly exposed their falsehood. Malthus's whole argument rests on the proposition that human populations increase geometrically, while their food supplies only increase sequentially. The key concept in Darwin's argument for natural selection is that plants and animals increase not at an arithmetical rate, as Malthus had supposed, but at a geometric rate, just as humans do. This is why one pair of elephants will have fifteen million descendants five hundred years later. It is also why, once farmers improve their methods and their land, the plants and animals they breed increase so rapidly they have been able to support a far larger population than in Malthus's day. What Malthus overlooked is that human beings are capable of adapting themselves to changing circumstances intelligently. [28] There was another irony. Whenever standards of living go up population numbers drop sharply. As William Howitt said of the Lancashire weavers in 1838 'It is generally the case that the most children are found in the poorest homes'. This is so much the case, in fact, that since they became wealthier as a consequence of joining the European Community, even Catholic countries such as Ireland, Italy and Spain are not even able to keep their populations at anywhere near replacement level. It was the deplorable social conditions that the Victorian middle classes were imposing on the poor that were themselves the condition of the population explosion that was so feared. And a yet further irony. The nineteenth century working classes did not outrun their food supplies. Instead, it was only the abundance of labouring hands that were available to dig the canals, build the railways, empty the chamber pots, man the looms, work the land and garrison India that made the middle classes so rich.

Perhaps the greatest irony of all is yet to come. In the twenty-first century it looks as if Malthus's prophecies will at last come true. But this is not because of any natural law that population will always outrun food supplies, as Malthus supposed. It is because of the climate change brought about, ultimately, by the industrial revolution with which *The Origin Of Species* was so intimately connected. Even now, theoretically at any rate, the earth could support the ten billion human beings that it is supposed the human race will, at its population peak, reach. If most people stopped eating meat and dairy products and lived only on plants, which incidentally would raise population even further by greatly improving general standards of health, it could easily be done. Mankind will starve not because of implacable natural laws but through a failure of human intelligence to adapt itself to the circumstances in which we now find ourselves. Our intelligence is failing us because we are stupefied by a falsifying myth, of which *The Origin Of Species,* it is the argument of this book, is at the very origin.

There was one other important influence on Darwin. But it did not come into full flower until he was actually on *The Beagle.*

(Endnotes)

1   N. Barlow ed. *The Autobiogaphy of Charles Darwin 1809-1882.* New York 1969. 119-120.
2   John Locke 1689 *An Essay Concerning Human Understanding* ed. Roger Woolhouse London Penguin 1997. p.105
3   *op. cit* p.462
4   *op. cit* p. 136
5   *op. cit.*p.135
6   *ibid*
7   William Paley *Natural Theology* Oxford Univ. Press 2006
8   *ibid* p. 69
9   op.cit. p.54.
10 op.cit p20
11 op.cit. p24
12 op.cit. p28
13 op. cit 104
14 op. cit. 237
15 op.cit 249
16 op. cit. 238
17 See Janet Browne *op.cit.* ch. 5
18 Michael Ruse 1979. *The Darwinian Revolution: Science Red in Tooth and Claw.* Chicago and London. Univ of Chicago Press ed. 1999 pp. 21-24
19 C. Darwin 1859 *The Origin Of Species.* London Penguin 1968 ed. P.117
20 Sylvan S. Schweber *The Origin of The Origin Revisited.* Journal of the History of Biology vol 10 no 2 (Fall 1977) pp. 229-316.
21 i*bid.*
22 See *Adam Smith: Essays On Philosophical Subjects.*ed. I.S. Ross. Indianapolos. Liberty
23 see Schweber *op.cit.*
24 Emma Rothschild *Adam Smith, Condorcet and the Enlightenment* pp. 56-71
25 quoted from Lord Cockburn by Rothschild

26 Adam Smith *Theory Of Moral Sentiments* Cambridge
    Univ. Pressd 2002 ed p.157
27 See Emma Rothschild 2001 *Economic Sentiments:
    Adam Smith, Condorcet and the Enlightenment*
    Harvard Harvard Univ Press
28 Gertrude Himmelfarb 1959. *Darwin and the
    Darwinian Revolution* ch. 15. Elephant paperbacks
    Chicago 1996

Chapter 5
Darwin's Fallacious Metaphors

Throughout *The Origin* Darwin is extremely confused as to whether he is speaking metaphorically or whether he isn't. In first introducing us to the concept of the struggle for existence he says, 'I should premise that I use the term Struggle for Existence in a large or metaphorical sense...'[1]. Yet he cannot possibly have intended that the central concepts that constitute his argument, natural selection, the war of nature and the struggle for existence itself, should be taken metaphorically. This was, after all, not primarily a work of literature but a work of science. The very same paragraph, which he begins by telling us he is speaking largely and metaphorically, goes on to say...' Two canine animals in a time of dearth may be truly said to struggle with each other which shall get food and live. But a plant on the edge of a desert is said to struggle for life against the drought: though more properly it should be said to be dependent on the moisture. A plant which annually produces a thousand seeds, of which on average only one comes to maturity, may be more truly said to struggle with the plants of the same and other kinds which already clothe the ground. The missletoe is dependent on the apple and a few other trees; but can only in a far-fetched sense be said to struggle with these trees; for if too many of these parasites grow on the same tree, it will languish and die. But several seedling missletoes, growing close together on the same branch, may be more truly said to struggle with each other. As the missletoe is disseminated by birds, its existence depends on birds; and it may metaphorically be said to struggle with other fruit-bearing plants, in order to tempt birds to devour and thus disseminate its seeds rather than those of other plants. In these several senses, which pass into each other, I use for convenience sake the general term of struggle for existence.'[2]

In other words, Darwin is using the concept of struggle for existence both literally and metaphorically. But it is often not clear which sense is intended. The senses vaguely 'pass into each other'. Sometimes Struggle for Existence gets capitals, at other times it doesn't. How can several misletoes growing on the same branch struggle with each other 'more truly'? More truly implies less metaphorically. How can you half-literally struggle? Why are misletoes that are competing with each other on the same tree literally struggling, while misletoes competing with other fruit-bearing plants struggle only metaphorically? This ambiguity in the use of metaphor is at the heart of the fallacy in *The Origin Of Species*. The whole purpose of the philosophical epistemology that Darwin had imbibed from Locke, and the heuristic scientific method he had been taught by Whewell and Herschell, was to release the truth-seeker from the distracting ambiguities of metaphor. That was what the scientific revolution of the seventeenth century was about. Stop talking about Dame Nature, take a look. But for Locke sense experience is itself a kind of metaphor or allegory, clothing and falsifying the real world of intellectually knowable law that lies behind it. For Herschell and Whewell the correct scientific procedure is, first, careful attention to sense data, second, the inductive discovery of regularities expressed in empirical laws, and, third, the use of deductive method to discover the abstract laws, the *verae causae* unknowable to sense but apprehensible by intellect, that lie behind and explain the empirical laws.

We can see this procedure being exactly and faithfully followed in the famous passage about the tangled bank that concludes Darwin's great work. 'It is interesting to contemplate an entangled bank, clothed with many plants of many kinds, with birds singing on the bushes, with various insects flitting about, and with worms crawling through the damp earth; and to reflect that these elaborately constructed forms, so different from each other, and dependent on each other in so complex a manner, have all been produced by laws acting around us. These laws, taken in the largest sense, being Growth with Reproduction; Inheritance which is almost implied by reproduction; Variability from the direct and indirect action of the external conditions of life; and from use and disuse; a Ratio of Increase so high as to lead to a Struggle for Life; and as a consequence to Natural Selection, entailing Divergence of Character and the Extinction of less improved forms. Thus from the war of nature, from famine and death...'[3]. Here we see, first, the close examination of the sensed life forms on the entangled bank; second, the observation of regularities: the empirically observed laws of growth with reproduction, inheritance, variability, and the ratio of increase. From this it is *deduced* that there must be a Struggle for Existence. From that it is further deduced that *as a consequence* there must be a law of Natural Selection, the biological equivalent of Newton's laws of motion, the ultimately explanatory and all-pervading law, the war of nature and famine and death.

In another less well known passage where he discusses an entangled bank, Darwin makes it even clearer that he intends natural selection, the struggle for existence and the war of nature to be taken not as metaphors but as the underlying laws that explain organic life. 'In the case of every species, many different checks, acting at different periods of life, and during different seasons or years, probably come into play; some one check or some few being generally the most potent, but all concurring in determining the average number or even the existence of the species. In some cases it can be shown that widely-different checks act on the same species in different districts. When we look at the plants and bushes clothing an entangled bank, we are tempted to attribute their proportional numbers and kinds to what we call chance. But how false a view is this! Every one has heard that when an American forest is cut down, a very different vegetation springs up; but it has been observed that the trees now growing on the ancient Indian mounds, in the Southern United States, display the same beautiful diversity and proportion of kinds as in the surrounding virgin forests. What a struggle between the several kinds of trees must here have gone on during long centuries, each annually scattering its seeds by the thousand; what war between insect and insect - between insects, snails, and other animals with birds and beasts of prey - all striving to increase, and all feeding on each other or on the trees or their seeds or seedlings, or on the other plants which first clothed the ground and thus checked the growth of the trees! Throw up a handful of feathers, and all must fall to the ground according to definite laws; but how simple is this problem compared to the action and reaction of the innumerable plants and animals which have determined, in the course of centuries, the proportional numbers and kinds of trees now growing on the old Indian ruins!'.[4]

In this passage struggle is no metaphor. It is the very dynamic of differentiation. The equivalent law to those determining the fallen position of the feathers is, in this case, the struggle itself. The struggle for existence is not merely a combat that is fought according to law. It *is* the law. War is not something which living things practise from time to time, it is their natural condition, which has determined their existence and brought them into being. Darwin so frequently presents to us the war of nature as an ultimate cause explaining the present state of organic life, there can be no doubt that in his mind actual, not merely imaginary, war plays a very large part indeed, both in nature's past history and its present economy. "Each organic being ... has to struggle for life and suffer great destruction".[5] It does not merely die. It is destroyed. "...from the war of nature, from famine and dearth...the production of the higher animals directly follows"[6]. "Battle within battle must ever be recurring with varying success". "Each being in the great and complex battle of life..."[7]. "...one species has been victorious over the other..." "...species and groups of species have tried to overmaster other species", as if the destruction of their competitors is not merely successful but deliberate.

War is no mere metaphor. It actually happens all the time. What Darwin is giving us in these entangled bank passages is an answer to Paley. Darwin's insects flitting about are echoes of Paley's wantonly happy gnats, weaving their airy patterns for the sheer joy of it. In his concluding paragraph Darwin is, first of all, reminding us of Paley's apparently happy world where birds sing, gnats play and worms crawl, and *then* showing us that behind this falsifyingly beguiling appearance there is a real world of quite opposite kind. To Paley's benign Deity, Darwin is opposing, as ultimate cause, the laws of nature. These laws are those of famine, war and death. It is here that we have the very essence of Darwin's fallacy. For the war of nature *is* a metaphor. Plants and animals do not fight wars. Far from being *verae causae,* famine and death are not the ultimate causes of anything, but merely empirical consequences. Darwin wasn't deducing these supposed laws. He was imagining them. He was projecting what only human beings are capable of doing onto nature.

The particular way in which Darwin presents Natural Selection to us involves even greater ambiguities than those implicit in his presentation of the Struggle for Existence. Ostensibly he was exposing Paley's mythical and metaphysical designing Deity, replacing him with scientifically attested laws of nature. But, most curiously, he does this in language implying not a physical replacement but an alternative metaphysical being. No Medieval poet celebrating Dame Nature could have committed the pathetic fallacy - or more accurately, perhaps, the unpathetic fallacy, for in Darwin's horrified account nature is emotionally quite unconcerned with the creatures she so brutally exterminates - with more enthusiasm. Natural Selection is 'a power incessantly ready for action'[8]. 'Man selects only for his own good; Nature only for the good of the being which she tends'[9]. 'It may be said that natural selection is daily and hourly scrutinizing, throughout the world, every variation, even the slightest; rejecting that which is bad, preserving and adding up all that is good.'[10] 'Natural selection will modify the structure of the young in relation to the parent, and of the parent in relation to the young. In social animals it will adapt the structure of each individual for the benefit of the community.....'[11] 'Though nature grants vast periods of time for the work of natural selection, she does not grant an indefinite period......if any one species does not become modified and improved in a corresponding degree with its competitors, it will soon be exterminated'[12]. If this is not language describing a cosmic designer it is difficult to know what is. There is, in fact, no meaning to the word select which does not involve the conscious, intelligent and deliberate choosing of one candidate and the rejection of another, with the corollary that selection is therefore the one thing nature cannot possibly do. Why did Darwin choose an expression for his central concept implying the precise opposite of what he meant?

Darwin's critics were not slow to catch on to the difficulties inherent in his anthropomorphic language. Sedgwick, among many others, took Darwin to task most sternly, almost vitriolically, on just this point. Wallace pointed out to Darwin that selection implied a selector and was therefore the antithesis of what he and Darwin had discovered. He wrote:

'Now I think this arises almost entirely from your choice of the term "Nat. Selection" & so constantly comparing it in its effects, to Man's selection, and also to your so frequently personifying Nature as "selecting", as "preferring", as "seeking only the good of the species" &c.&c. To the few, this is as clear as daylight, & beautifully suggestive, but to many it is evidently a stumbling block. I would therefore suggest to you the possibility of entirely avoiding this source of misconception in your great work, (if not now too late) & also in any future editions of the "Origin", and I think it may be done without difficulty & very effectually by adopting Spenser's term (which he generally uses in preference to Nat. Selection) viz. "Survival of the fittest" '.[13]

* * *

Although Darwin did somewhat grudgingly appease Wallace to the extent of using Survival of the Fittest occasionally in *The Descent Of Man,* he resolutely refused to give up his predilection for Natural Selection. He replied to his critics in the preface to the third edition of *The Origin:*

'In the literal sense of the word, no doubt, natural selection is a false term; but whoever objected to chemists speaking of the elective affinities of the various elements? – and yet an acid cannot strictly be said to elect the base with which it in preference combines. It is said that I speak of natural selection as an active power or Deity; but who objects to an author speaking of the attraction of gravity as ruling the movements of the planets? Every one knows what is meant and implied by such metaphorical expressions: and they are almost necessary for brevity. So again it is difficult to avoid personifying the word Nature. But I mean by Nature, only the aggregate action and product of many natural laws, and by laws the sequence of events as ascertained by us. With a little familiarity such superficial objections will be forgotten.'

If Darwin was not being disingenuous here he was certainly being myopic. In this case, most certainly, not everybody did know what was meant. That was precisely why his friends and supporters were so alarmed by his insistent use of the term. In the way he presented natural selection as a law, Darwin clearly did not merely mean 'the sequence of events as ascertained by us'. He presents natural selection not only as a descriptive law, Herschel's first and lesser empirical kind of law, but as an ultimate explanation, a true *vera causa*. A merely descriptive law, 'the sequence of events as ascertained by us', would imply, given Darwin's adherence to the Herschell-Whewell understanding of methodology in science, that there was a further explanation for the sequence of events, which, if it were not the designing deity he was denying, could only be law taken in a much more radical sense that the mere observation of sequences in events. Either natural selection is no metaphor, in which case nature is literally personified, or it is, in which case, Darwin is implicitly admitting, it amounts to little more than the superficial observation of regularities. Chemists may speak of elements electing each other and cosmologists of gravity ruling planets. But they do not use metaphors that imply the precise opposite of what they mean. The meanings they give to these terms are so factually limited and precise – some elements combine with others to form compounds, masses moving in space cannot avoid the pull of gravity – they have in effect withdrawn them from their original metaphorical context.

* * *

This is not the case with natural selection. Darwin could quite easily have encompassed the meaning of the actual facts he had discovered – that under circumstances of scarce resources specific varieties better adapted to their environment are more likely to survive and hand on their fortunate attributes to their descendants, until eventually through many such small incremental changes entirely new species are formed - by employing some such expression as Speciation By Differential Survival. But in that case all the rich quasi-divine paraphernalia of ambiguity that surrounded the concept of natural selection in vague clouds, all the relentless daily and hourly scrutinizing, the rejecting and preserving, the granting of great periods of time, the ruthless exterminations, the warfare, the seemingly teleological intention of producing a better organism, the careful tending, the adapting, the modifying, the intrinsically intentional activities so inescapably reminiscent of the plant breeders from whom Darwin had originally taken his metaphor – all of this becomes redundant. Why was Darwin, in the face of so much criticism, so insistent on continuing to use an expression that was not only confusing but compromised the very essence of what he said he meant? It is a question I shall try to answer in the course of the following chapters.

Darwin's errors arose from the constriction of his philosophical background. Just as Locke's epistemology misled him into discounting sensed phenomena, so that he was always looking for hidden abstract laws to explain everything about physical appearances and found no explanations in the appearances themselves, so Comte and Quetelet fatally misled him into misunderstanding the importance of chance. It is often thought that Darwin replaced Paley's intelligibly designed universe with an unintelligible random one. In fact his intention was precisely the opposite. 'I have hitherto sometimes spoken' he tells us at the beginning of the chapter called, significantly, Laws of Variation, 'as if the variations – so common and multiform in organic beings under domestication and in a lesser degree in those in a state of nature – had been due to chance. This, of course, is a wholly incorrect expression...' That 'of course' tells us a lot about the assumptions Darwin was making. Just as his lack of acquaintance with the Aristotelian tradition led him to ignore the importance of studying the form of organic beings in order to understand life, so his view of determination and chance was impoverished by lack of acquaintance with Aristotle's teaching on the relation of form to matter. The great excitement that Darwin had caught at Cambridge from Henslow, Sedgwick and Whewell, and from first reading about Herschell's ideas and then meeting the great man at the Cape during the voyage of *The Beagle,* was the rapid extension of the empire of science that was happening during the early nineteenth century. Ultimately, and much of it soon, *everything* would be rationally explained. The comprehensive intelligibility that Newton had discovered in inorganic forms was now to be extended to life. As a result, Darwin had little notion of Aristotle's understanding of the importance of unintelligibility.

According to the determinism Darwin inherited from Quetelet and Laplace nothing in the universe is the result of accident. The statistical regularities, so useful to insurance companies and actuaries, are as orderly and patterned as they are because, despite appearances, even the world of sublunary accident is not immune to the operation of law. They are, in fact, examples of Herschell's first kind of law, the establishment of empirical regularities in apparently random phenomena, which, heuristically speaking, will eventually lead to the *verae causae* that explain the empirical laws. We only think that the dice falls on a six by chance because we do not have enough information about the laws which controlled the velocity of the throw, the weight of the dice, the air pressures in the smokey gambling den, the excited condition of the gambler that resulted in the theoretically computable varying energy levels of his shaking hand etc, etc. If we did, we would be able to predict its fall as accurately as we can predict a coming eclipse. Darwin thought of the variations that lead to speciation in just this light. It was his constant complaint that he and everyone else at that time knew so little about the laws of variation that he was driven to talk about variation *as if* it were a matter of chance. But this was simply the result of ignorance.

Aristotle's view is a completely different one. For him form and matter are as relative to each other as left and right, form is intelligible and matter relatively unintelligible. Thus intelligibility and unintelligibility are intrinsically linked. When an artist makes a statue the statue is the form and the bronze out of which he makes it the matter. In imposing his idea on bronze he has brought it into a higher state of intelligibility. But the bronze is itself a form composed out of lower material elements, the copper and tin which were used to mix it. Because it is a more complex form than the elements out of which it was composed it, too, is more intelligible than they are. And so we go on down the scale, with each level being an enactment of the material potentiality in the level below it, which is itself an enactment, in Aristotle's sense, of the material potentiality of an even lower level, until in the end we reach sheer potentiality, what he calls prime matter. What he means is the sheer *thatness* of things, the sheer absolutely unintelligible fact that they're there, what Bernard Lonergan calls the empirical residue.[14] Imagine you find two stones in your garden. If you took a great deal of trouble you could find out more and more fully, by studying the cosmological, geological, social and historical sciences, and perhaps in the end more or less completely, how they got there. But the *fact* that they are there, the 'there they are in your garden', is in itself unintelligible. It's just a given.

If Darwin had had some sympathy with this point of view he would have approached the problem of the origin of species quite differently. Ironically, he was in fact seeking the direct opposite of the randomness with which he is so often thought to have slain God. What he missed was the sheer happeningness of what happens. There is a cognitive logic which explains to us the rationally apprehensible processes which led to the development of the human brain. Similarly there is a meteorological logic which enables us to understand why the African Rift Valley dried out during the Pleistocene. Both of these we can understand. But what we cannot understand is the absolutely crucial condition that propelled human evolution: the change in weather conditions *happened* to coincide with the existence of a creature which had developed in such a way that its brain was now capable of sudden and decisive increase in size. Similarly, when the climate dries out and fruit trees get scarcer monkeys eat the fruit first because, as it happens, they can digest it raw, for physiological reasons that are nothing to do with climate, so it is not there when the apes arrive. As a result monkeys often survive and apes frequently do not, and there are therefore more monkeys in the world today than apes. But this is not a law. It is simply a train of events that has happened many, many times. What explains that today there are only four species of great apes, but many species of monkeys, is the fact that the fruit just wasn't there.

* * *

Soon there will only be three species of great apes left. The orang utans are soon going to die out because of the destruction of the rainforests where they live. This destruction is, it is true, as stupid and wanton and greedy as could be imagined. But it is at least intelligible. It is occurring within a schedule of meaning: the desire of loggers to make money by cutting down trees to make space for growing bio-fuel, so that they can sell it as oil gets scarcer and more costly. The orangs are also operating within an intelligible schedule of meaning. They want to stay alive by finding food in the rain forests. They have a purpose and the loggers have a purpose. But there is no *overall* schedule of meaning. There is no greater scheme of purposes within which these lesser purposes are operating. It's just bad luck on the orangs that they happen to be sharing their world with human beings who now want to use bio-fuels. The humans want to use bio-fuels because they invented petrol engines but now oil is getting scarce, and they invented petrol engines because previously they had invented steam engines. But there is no continuous network of intelligibility connecting the searching for food of the orangs in the rain forest with Watt's invention of the steam engine. It's just, as Rumsfeld said, that stuff happens. But, in spite of the popular misconception that this was just what he was overthrowing, Darwin *was* looking for a greater overall schedule of meaning. It is what he meant by natural selection. But there is no such overall schedule. The one thing nature cannot do is select.

We should think of evolution as if it were a cricket match. The batsmen return to the pavilion as they are given out in accordance with the laws of the game. This game too is played in accordance with laws. They are those of physics and bio-chemistry. But the actual story of this particular game isn't a law. It's just what happened in this particular game. There is nothing lawful *in the game itself.* Natural selection, strictly speaking, is the equivalent in biology of the merely mechanical, and in itself unintelligible, condition in cricket that when one batsman fails and is given out it creates the opportunity for a new one, who may fare better, to come in. But the sheer fact that a failed batsman is replaced by another one *in itself* explains nothing: neither why the first was given out nor whether the replacement may have a technique better suited to the conditions. Darwin mistook the pattern for the explanation.

The autumn of 2000 happened to be very wet. In York, a city very liable to flood, they have a rain gauge in the middle of the city that records the levels the water reached in exceptional years, when flooding reached historic levels. In 2000 the water came up to the very highest point on the gauge. Some houses

171

were so badly damaged they had to be demolished. People who were well insured were, it is true, inconvenienced, but their houses were replaced, and they went on to benefit from the general increase in house prices that happened after 2000. They were in the happy position, too, of being able to hand on their advantage to their descendants. But those who were not insured lost everything. In their case, their children found themselves with no hope, even, of ever getting on the housing ladder. There were winners and losers. But we don't say Nature Selected the highest point on the gauge. It just happened to be a very wet autumn.

Suppose you landed on an uninhabited island and found a neat row of shoes. They go from very crude forms, simple flipflops made of a cork sole and a twine thong, then ones with wooden heels, then ones with leather uppers but also fastened with a thong, and finally ones where the uppers have had holes punched in them for laces. These latter seem to be the final design, but at this level there are a number of different variations, some that are heavy brogues, light ones that would be good for running in, and some very elegant ones with stiletto heels. On investigating the island further, you find odd scraps here and there that seem to have belonged to failed attempts to produce shoes: a bit of sole made of woven grass, a detached heel made from compressed seaweed, uppers made from canvas, a stiletto heel that was literally an adapted knife blade Why did the ones in the neat row survive while the others did not? It seems reasonable to assume that it was because, at every level, they worked better than the other available versions, as the environments in which, and the purposes for which, people wanted to wear shoes changed. There is a sense in which the better adaptation to their environments of the preserved shoes, a process brought about in this case by intelligent agents but not independent in itself and certainly not itself intelligent, is an important principle explaining their survival. If we were speaking extremely poetically, we might even say that adaptation to environment selected the shoes in the neat row. But we wouldn't dream of saying that it designed them. That it was the *only* reason why there was a row of shoes and not just bits of cork, wood and leather lying around. In the case of the shoes we would have no doubt that they were the product of an intelligent designer. Nevertheless, the role of adaptation to environment is exactly the same in the case of the shoes as it is in the case of living organisms, and is nothing to do with whether there was a designer or not. Natural selection explains the differential survival of forms *that are already in existence for some other reason.* But it only ever works at any one point. It shows why chimpanzees survived better than other cruder chimpanzee- like alternatives and *then* why modern humans survived better than Neanderthals. But it does not give us an *overall* explanation. Natural selection is one damn survival after another. It doesn't explain the existence of the forms themselves. Darwin confused coincidental condition with formal cause.

Imagine a narrow valley with escarpments on both sides made out of different kinds of rock, one hard and the other soft. During long ages pieces of rock have broken off on both sides and rolled down the slopes to form ridges and barriers in flatter places. On both sides the barriers have become impenetrable, except for narrow gaps which haven't yet been filled. Because one type of rock is softer than the other, the pieces that break off on that side weather much more quickly, and fall through the gaps to reach the valley below. There they silt up to dam the valley, with dramatic effects on the flora and fauna that live there. But there is no principle of Natural Gappiness, selecting the soft rock and thereby explaining the rich life in the valley below. The rocks are not engaged in a bitter struggle for existence to see which can get through the gaps. The scientific explanations that make *each aspect* of this situation intelligible, why one set of rocks is hard and the other soft, why the gaps are in just the places they are, are highly complex. But the whole network of coincidences that make the rich life of the valley possible – one set of rocks being soft, the gaps being just where they are, both sides having plateaus where barriers formed, the fact that the river in the valley below was flowing placidly and slowly enough to allow the silt to form dams – was in itself not intelligible. It just happened that way.

* * *

Suppose a thrush happens to have developed a gene that gives it better eyesight, and therefore makes it better at finding worms. In hard winters when worms are scarce its eyesight enables it to survive, whereas other thrushes not so fortuitously blessed starve and die. What caused it to survive was its better eyesight. It was not the famine and death that killed the other thrushes. Darwin got it the wrong way round. There are no laws of famine and death that explain organic evolution. What he missed was the happeningness of what happens. There are intelligible scientific laws that explain life. But they operate against a background of unintelligible fortuitous chance. There is, as it were, an entropy in the organic sciences just as there is in the inorganic ones. There is an empirical residue. Comte and Quetelet and Darwin all missed this, in itself unintelligible, fact. Aristotle didn't.

There is no natural selection, or at least none in the sense Darwin meant. Nor is there a struggle for existence. Animals and plants struggle each individually *to exist*. They do not struggle in order to achieve some overall abstract state called existence. There is a crucial difference here between natural selection and Newton's laws of motion. There must be some sense in which Newton's laws are either out there or, at least, as near as dammit out there, as the mental triangle whose hundred and eighty degreeness Euclid has proved to you is as near as dammit to the one in your geometry book. Some mathematicians, the implicit Platonists, think that abstract mathematical truths have a kind of objective existence. Others, the grumpy Humeans, tend to the idea that mathematical abstractions are only convenient mental generalizations that refer to myriads of instances. But even the grumpy Humeans have to admit that the concentrated mathematical generalizations, that they believe the laws of science to be, are in practice as near as dammit to Platonish abstractions. Or at least, in order to understand them we have to treat them as if they are. You can't fly a man to the moon without understanding Newton's laws, but you can contemplate Newton's laws as if they had nothing to do with flying men to the moon. And to get to the stage of using them to fly men to the moon, you had first to abstract them from observed phenomena and treat them as if they were independent immaterial entities in order to understand them.

* * *

The struggle for existence is different. Existence itself, as opposed to a myriad instances of existing, is not something which is happening out there in any absolute, or even near as dammit, sense. There is no mathematical formula you can write down, as you can write one down for Newton's laws. It is an abstraction that only enters into the world with the arrival of human beings. Existence is a generalized idea drawn from a multitude of individuals who, as it happened, existed. It exists in the mind only. Or if it does exist in some reality out there, then it implies the existence of just that superhuman intelligence which would alter Darwin's theories completely. According to Aquinas God's essence *is* his existence. But such scholastic conceptions are a million miles away from Darwin's thought world. If there is no superhuman intelligence, then existence did not exist until human beings came along to conceive of the idea. But there must be some sense in which Newton's laws of motion existed before Newton discovered them, or even before humans arrived on the scene, or even before the solar system was formed. Darwin's error was to treat what were in fact merely descriptive empirical laws as if they were *verae causae.* There is no struggle for existence in nature ruling the activities of animals and plants, as there is a law of gravity ruling the planets. There are just a myriad of plants and animals, turning their leaves towards the sun, looking for mates, building nests and doing all the other things plants and animals do as they struggle to exist.

* * *

Nor is there any competition in nature. Competitions are deliberately structured human artifices carefully arranged so that there are winners and losers. The Association Football League Premiership is a competition. Biology is not. Animals don't compete. They just look for the next rival to fight or the next nut to store. Species which disappear don't lose. They just disappear. To return to the cricket analogy, each batsman when given out has to return to the pavilion, under the pressure of the law that only two batsmen can be at the wicket at the same time. But the one who replaces him is not competing with the one who has been given out. On the contrary, both are seeking to contribute to their team's score. In just this way each species, each animal, makes its contribution to the glory of life until its time is over and it is replaced by another. But it has not been exterminated by nature. It has simply failed to cope with the bowling. Nor, in nature, is there any Survival of the Fittest, in the sense that Darwin and Spenser meant. Not only because for animals there are no abstractions such as existence or survival, but also because there are no fittest. *Comparative scale* is a human artifice too. Of course, in a non-human world the best adapted animals would still be the ones that survived and handed on their attributed to their offspring. But imagine a world in which there are as yet no intelligent human beings nor, if most Darwinian biologists are right, no God. Who would make comparisons? Fit, fitter and fittest are judgments. In such a world there would be no judgments, just the fact that some survived and some did not. But the survivors didn't survive *because* they were the fittest. They survived because of quite other laws, mostly physiological and genetic, that enabled them to survive. 'The fittest' is simply the name we give to this process. But names don't cause anything, any more than calling rising prices inflation causes prices to rise. Natural selection is not a cause of evolution. It is a consequence.

What causes evolution are hidden changes occurring genetically, and intelligibly, deep within the molecular structures of plants and animals, emanating ultimately from a quantum level, expressing themselves in a world ruled by classical law where, unintelligibly, two different things cannot occupy the same place at the same time. The consequence is that animals in whom the more advantageous mutations occurred survive and the others do not. The survivors did not survive because nature selected them. They survived because the molecular changes that had occurred within them happened to be the ones needed in a fortuitously changing environment. They did not survive because their survival was itself a causal law explaining their survival, any more than we say that a man escaped drowning because he escaped drowning rather than because he was a strong swimmer. But Darwin did treat natural selection as if it were a cause. He did not deliberately impose the social structure of Victorian Britain onto nature. But he did think about nature in the ways that Victorian Britons thought. Thus he exemplified Adam Smith's dictum that scientists first imagine the truths that they discover within the imaginative framework of the society within which they live. Darwin looked at living things *as if* they were the winners and losers of Victorian England. The first fallacy was the distortion of Adam Smith's ideas by the early Victorian economists. The second was the mythologizing of these ideas onto nature by Darwin. Then, trebling the fallacy, the Victorians re-assured themselves that the ways in which they thought were infallibly correct because they were rooted in nature, and had now been scientifically shown to be so.

Suppose Darwin had not been the son of a middle class Victorian family with close connections to the highly competitive commercial world of pottery, a family who before all things believed in free trade, and feared above all things an over-populated and starving insurrectionary working class, and who, dismayed by their scion's dismal failure to embrace the medical profession, fell back in desperation on that final standby to provide a living for worthless sons, the divinity course at Cambridge. Suppose he had instead been sent to Weimar to study biology under Goethe who, incidentally, did not die until 1832. How much then the enrichment of organic form rather than competition might have been at the centre of his vision. Or suppose he had been as familiar with the subtle thinking in *Summa Theologiae Prima Pars Quaestio 8,* where Aquinas considers the proposition 'On the Immanence of God in the Universe', as he was with Paley's theological watch maker. How differently Darwin might have thought if he had understood Aquinas's insight that design does not happen outside things but within things. How much better Aquinas and Aristotle chime here with what we now know about genes, nucleotides and quantum physics than does Paley. Or suppose Darwin had been born a Hindu. How the random effervescences of life would have illustrated the divine play of Brahman in creation.   It is only by accident, ironically enough, that the theory of evolution has evolved as it has. But try thinking it through in a frame other than that of Anglo-Saxon empiricism. How much richer its myth then becomes.

(Endnotes)

1   Charles Darwin 1859 *The Origin Of Species*
     London John Murray Penguin ed. 1968. Ch 5
2   *op. cit* p.116
3   *op. cit* ch.14
4   ibid *op.cit*p.125
5   ibid
6   *op.cit* p.459
7   ibid p.130
8   ibid p.115
9   ibid. p.132
10   ibid. p.133
11   ibid. p.135
12   ibid p.147
13   Quoted in Janet Browne *op, cit.* vol 2 p. 312
14   Bernard Lonergan 1961 *Insight: A Study Of*
     Human Understanding. Toronto. Univ of Toronto ed. 1992

Chapter 6
The Mythical *Origin*

The Origin Of Species is not only one of the foundation texts of modern science, it is also one of the great works of English letters. Through ambiguity in his use of metaphor Darwin was not only able to engage the intellect by his presentation of natural selection as an irrefutable *vera causa* – because all organic forms breed up to their resources there *must* be a struggle for existence and therefore there *must* be natural selection – he was also able, uniquely in a scientific work, to invade and compel the imagination. As happens with only the greatest and most classic creations of literature, Natural Selection – the capitals are Darwin's – has entered into the fabric of our feeling life. Ever the theologian he so very nearly became, Darwin writes Paley in reverse. He disposes of Paley's God but then re-imagines him. Whereas Paley's Deity was male, Darwin's is female. Whereas Paley's benign creator walks in the garden in the cool of the evening, smiling delightedly at the happy contrivances he has made, Darwin's is grimly efficient, cruel and heartless. Paley's God creates by contriving, Darwin's by exterminating. Darwin penetrates far below the conscious levels of our everyday working minds into regions of dream and fantasy. He turns Dame Nature from an Ideal into a Terrible Mother. Like a terrifying dark bird, in its unresting zeal to eliminate failures Natural Selection hovers mercilessly over its killing fields, scrutinizing them minutely with its baleful glare, devouring the feeble and the slow. Like an SS doctor on the ramp at Auschwitz, in its relentless search for a superior organism it selects the old and the useless for immediate extermination, and assigns the fit to a hellish struggle for survival. Like the fossils that verified it, Darwin excavated Natural Selection from deeply archaic and profoundly buried levels. It is our worst nightmare scientifically attested.

In the western liberal mythology that has been woven about the reception of *The Origin,* the scientists are presented as brave heroes of light, Darwin's shining knights gathered round their enfeebled vomiting king, triumphantly fighting the forces of theological darkness. They win of course, for in myths heroes always do. Yet it wasn't actually like that. In fact it was almost, though not quite, the opposite. On the scientific side, the scientists, even Darwin's closest associates, always had doubts about natural selection. His hero Sir John Herschel, to his disciple's considerable mortification, dismissed natural selection as "the law of higgledy piggledy"[1]. All three of the intimate friends – Lyell, Huxley and Hooker - to whom he revealed his theory during the long years of secret incubation that preceded the publication of *The Origin*, rejected it right up to 1859. Hooker told Darwin that the theory was so naïve he needed to study more biology. Like the modest gentleman he was, Darwin humbly accepted the criticism and put the theory on hold while he spent eight years studying barnacles. Lyell never accepted the theory *in toto* and was still holding out for a special creation of man as late as1868, and even after that was a grudging and reluctant convert.[2] After 1859 Hooker was Darwin's most faithful supporter. As a botanist he saw that the distribution of Australian plants and of Arctic plants in North America and Greenland could only be explained by natural selection.[3] But Hooker too confessed that 'conviction was forced upon an unwilling convert'[4] Darwin wrote to Hooker, 'Such men as you and Lyell thinking that I make too much of a Deus of Natural Selection is a conclusive argument against me'.[5]

* * *

Even Darwin's bulldog never really believed the theory whole-heartedly. Huxley was always suspicious of Darwin's analogy with artificial selection and often preceded talks he gave about Darwinian evolution, and they were many for his promotion of Darwin's ideas was tireless, with a disclaimer pointing out that natural selection was still only an unproved theory. Ironically, nobody could have been more aware of the poisonous barb in Wilberforce's jibing taunt about Huxley's grandparents being apes than Huxley himself. Deeply alarmed that Darwin's theory had released the ape into the drawing room, in the later years of the century Huxley became the most formidable opponent of Social Darwinism in England. The scientists rallied round Darwin because, in the simplifications of battle, they saw the controversy aroused by the publication of *The Origin* as their great opportunity to assert the pre-eminence and independence of science, and because they believed that not only Darwin but the theory of evolution itself, and by implication science's warrant to investigate life, was under attack. They also found Darwin's materialism invaluable in resisting what Huxley described as 'the metaphysical hocus pocus' of Owen's homologies. The defence of *The Origin* was also a battle to save Baconian empiricism. But the attacks from the scientists continued. The co-founder of evolution by natural selection, Wallace, came to disagree utterly with Darwin's view that natural selection explained human evolution just as much as it explained any other. The Cambridge mathematician William Hopkins pointed out that whereas hitherto unknown facts had been deduced from Newton's *Principia* and then confirmed in the real world, no new fossils could be deduced from *The Origin,* nor of the existing ones were there enough to put his theory beyond doubt. Darwin was forced to agree.[6]

Somewhat complacently Darwin had written to Lyell 'You will think me very conceited... because I find so many young and middle aged truly good workers in different branches, either wholly or partly accepting my views'.[7] But Darwin's self-confessed conceit was misplaced. As the century progressed the younger scientists disassociated themselves more and more from Darwin's theory. William Thomson, later Lord Kelvin and already a leading cosmological physicist, dealt a body blow by asserting that the age of the earth was not nearly great enough to allow the slow evolutionary change necessitated by Darwin's theory. It was a criticism Darwin was never able to answer. More seriously still, a Scottish engineer called Fleeming Jenkin called attention to the problem of blending in Darwin's theory of inheritance. Can anyone believe, he wrote, that if a single white man became king of a native island and in the struggle for existence killed many blacks and had many offspring, that in time the whole population of the island would become white? The inherited characteristics of a single ancestor, be they never so favourable, would gradually disappear as they blended with those of the majority. Darwin attempted to answer the charge with his theory of pangenesis. Every cell in an organism, he imagined, produces tiny gemmules, as he called them, which circulated in the blood and were transmitted by parents through sex to their offspring. They could resist blending by lying dormant for many generations. Pangenesis was not received with any great ovation. One of its few enthusiastic supporters, Darwin's cousin Francis Galton, the founder of eugenics, sought to prove it by injecting blood from a black and white rabbit into a silver-grey, which was put to breed with another silver-grey. The cousins waited with baited breath to see whether the silver grey doe would produce an offspring with black and white markings, which, to their triumphant satisfaction, it did. It was only later that they discovered that this was a common occurrence among rabbits.[8] By the mid-seventies even Darwin had semi-abandoned his theory and fallen back on Lamarck.

On the other hand, despite the great howl of rage from some of their most prominent spokesmen, most religious believers rapidly accommodated themselves to Darwinism. One of the many paradoxes of the controversy in 1859 is that it was, almost wholly, not about the origin of species but the creation of man, about which Darwin had said nothing except for his enigmatic 'light will be thrown…' It was the monkey question that inflamed the passions. Why was Darwin being attacked for something he had not even said? The curious thing was, the literal truth of the Bible was being attacked from within religion by clergymen, arguing fiercely about the meaning of biblical texts, even more than from without by Darwin. Lyell had already undermined the account of creation in Genesis with his *Principles of Geology.* Published shortly after *The Origin, Essays And Reviews* written by seven liberal clergymen, dealt further blows. One of them, Baden-Powell, sided openly with natural selection. At much the same time Bishop Colenso of Natal wrote a book pointing out that an elementarily mathematical reading of the Old Testament would imply that one man's public address had been heard by two million people, that six men had 2,748 sons between them, and every priest had to eat eighty eight pigeons a day.[9] Many religious believers, even most, had already quietly accepted evolution well before 1859. The anonymous *Vestiges,* asserting creation by natural evolution and not by divine miracle and published in 1844, had found little favour with scientists but had been immensely popular with the general public. Tennyson's *In Memoriam,* with its memorable picture of nature red in tooth and claw, and its injunction to mankind to work out from itself 'the beast, and let the ape and tiger die', sat happily on many a clergyman's shelf.

Asa Gray, Darwin's fervently Christian supporter in America, was wholly supportive. The Reverend Charles Kingsley's reaction was so favourable and delighted Darwin so much he included Kingsley's encomium in the frontispiece of the second edition. This Christian understanding of *The Origin,* taking the view that God could as well have used evolution to create man as miracle, and indeed that the uniformity of nature was more consonant with the rationality of the divine intention than an irrational interruption of it, soon began to appeal to many fence-sitters. Of the reviews, those in the Catholic periodicals *The Dublin Review* and *The Rambler* were far from hostile. *The Dublin Review,* in fact, congratulated Darwin on rebuking the irreligious views of earlier scientists who had dared to question mankind's descent from a single original pair.[10] *The Saturday Review,* a bastion of orthodoxy, was most respectful in its dissent. The extremely hostile piece in *The Quarterly Review* by Wilberforce was mainly huff and puff. Another extremely unfavourable, angry and anonymous review in *The Spectator* was written, Darwin rightly suspected, by Sedgwick. But since Sedgwick's geology – 'those dreadful hammers' wrote Ruskin – had done as much as anything to discredit Genesis, Sedgwick was hardly in a position to complain. Owen's review in *The Edinburgh Review,* again anonymous but so vainly self-serving no-one in the know had any doubt as to who had written it, confusingly both attacked the idea of natural selection and claimed credit for having thought of it first.   Why did the religious critics not make more of the doubts, and the lack of evidence, that so worried the scientific supporters?[11]   By 1871, when Darwin published *The Descent Of Man,* putting forward the account of an entirely natural origin for human beings that he had not dared to express in 1859, he was met with universal approval, not least from clergymen who by this time were only too anxious to display their up-to-date breadth of view.   Darwin was finally claimed by religion as one of its own and buried in Westminster Abbey.   And there was one more curious thing.   This book, that everybody was talking about, had become by 1861 when Darwin's publisher Murray brought out the third edition, the most famous book in the world after the Bible.   But how many people had actually read it?   Murray's print run for the third edition was 2000, which brought the total number of copies sold up to 7000.[12]   That wasn't a bad number for a scientific book.   But this was the most controversial book in the world, and assuredly there were far more than 7000 people talking about what they had not read.   Contrastingly, *The Descent Of Man* was in profit almost immediately.   There is much to suggest that the reception of *The Origin* was not all that it seemed.

In the famous debate at Oxford, amidst people shouting hysterically and undergraduates chanting Mawnkee Mawnkee, it was almost as if Wilberforce deliberately set Huxley up to deliver the most celebrated sound-bite of the nineteenth century – though needless to say that wasn't what Huxley actually said[13] - 'I had rather have an ape for a grandfather than a bishop'. 'The Lord has delivered him into my hands', said Huxley to a neighbour as he rose to reply. It was almost as if some religious believers made so great a noise of complaint to cover up what they profoundly and guiltily were already accepting. Indeed, what is most striking about the hysterically hostile reactions is that nobody attempted to defend the central thing that Genesis actually says about nature, that it is good, but without exception tacitly accepted Darwin's view of nature as ruthlessly violent and competitive. Every society defines its understanding of itself and its relation to the natural world in a creation myth. The Victorians had embarked on bringing about the greatest change in mankind's relationship with nature since the agricultural revolution, perhaps indeed since

194

the appearance of self-consciousness, and it was for that reason that they already had problems about their own received myth of creation. For the first time in human history nature was being seen not primarily as a wonder to be contemplated but as a resource to be used and exploited. Genesis was no longer of any use, in fact it was worse, it had become a skeleton at the feast, a deep source of guilt and anxiety. The problem was that Genesis did not recommend getting rich at nature's expense but, as God did, loving the natural things he had made. Genesis was therefore now a problem, even more for Christians than for secularists, but most of all for clergymen, for almost to a man the clergy were enthusiastic supporters of the middle-class project to become rich and then richer still. The Gospel's injunction to care for the poor did not, for example, prevent Whewell from supporting the corn laws, for Trinity College's wealth and his own income were dependent on high rents.

There are two versions of the creation in Genesis, but neither of them throws a very favourable light on the great Victorian undertaking. The first version, that of Chapter One, is in fact almost the last part of the Old Testament to have been written. It was composed by priests during the Babylonian exile and is heavily influenced by the Babylonian creation myth, the *Enuma Elish.* In the Babylonian story the male god Apsu and the female goddess Tiamat, or Chaos, have offspring who are very unruly and 'trouble Tiamat's belly'. Angered by their behaviour, Tiamat vows to destroy them and sets out to do so with her son Kingu placed at the head of an army of monsters. This greatly alarms the lesser gods, who then turn to one of their number, Ea's son Marduk, to save them from Tiamat. A great battle ensues. Marduk arms himself with the lightning and the four winds which he carries in a net, and sets forth in his storm chariot to fight Chaos. He caught Tiamat in his net, and as she opened her mouth blew the four winds into her stomach. She grew so huge she couldn't move. He pierced her heart with an arrow, smashed her skull with a mace, and split her body open 'like a shellfish'. The army of monsters fled. Out of Tiamat's body he made the earth. With half of it he made the sky with sun and moon. With the other half he set the earth in order and made the animals and plants. But he was now tired. So he decided to put Kingu to death, and out of his blood he fashioned the first human being.[14] He made man as a slave so that the gods could rest.

The re-fashioning of this story in Genesis is extremely striking. The Hebrew word for chaos is closely related to the Babylonian Tiamat. But whereas in the Babylonian myth Marduk kills his mother with the greatest violence, in the literal Hebrew Lord God hovers protectively over her. Marduk's terrible wind becomes Lord God's gentle *ruach,* which means both wind and spirit. Lord God fashions the world out of chaos not by smashing his mother to pieces but by breathing his spirit, his *ruach,* into her face and making love to her. Like Marduk he creates the world in six stages, each of which delights him beyond measure. Finally he creates man not to be a slave but the free image of himself. At this point the text bursts into song. Like Lord God himself the human, taken from the *humus,* the earth, is a free person. 'So Lord God made man in his own image, in the image of God he created him; male and female he created them'. On the last day he rests and contemplates the goodness of everything he has made.

The second account, in Chapter Two, is even more a song of love. Yahweh first made the earth (*ha-adama)*, but as yet the earth was barren. To solve this problem, he took a handful of earth and fashioned an earth-creature (*ha-adam).*

Because the earth was barren
And that was because there was as yet no earth
creature to serve the earth
He took a handful of dust from the earth and
breathed life into its nostrils

As yet the earth creature had no sex. Yahweh made
a garden for the earth creature to live in and called it
the Garden of Delight because, literally in the Hebrew,
designing it had given him so much pleasure. Yahweh
put plants into the garden, so that the earth creature
would be satisfied both aesthetically and physically.
They were good to look at and good to eat. He told the
earth creature to look after the garden.

Yahweh took *ha-adam* and put it in the Garden
of Eden
To till it and keep it.

The Hebrew word *'bd,* to till, is extremely rich in
its meanings, implying among other things to care for,
to reverence, to respect, to love, even to worship. Most
especially Yahweh planted two trees, the tree of life
and the tree of knowledge. The only condition he laid
down was that the earth creature should not eat of the

tree of knowledge of good and evil. 'The forbidden tree spells limits to human dominion. Nature itself has also God-given independence'.[15]

But there was a problem. The earth creature was lonely.

> And Yahweh God said
> It is not good for *ha-adam* to be alone
> I will make for it a companion corresponding to it.
> And Yahweh formed from *ha-adama*
> Every beast of the field and every bird of the heavens
> And he brought each to *ha-adam* to see what it would call each one.

Yahweh brings the birds and animals that he has fashioned out of the earth to the earth-creature in order that they might be its friends, and the earth creature gives them names, not the names of species but personal ones, the kind of names that you might give to pets. Yahweh gave the earth creature dominion over the animals he had made and told the earth-creature to look after them. But the earth-creature was still lonely. Yahweh God thought about the problem very deeply.

This time he didn't fashion a new kind of creature out of the earth. He put *ha-adam* into a deep sleep and opening its body he refashioned it. What was still one he made into two. When *ha-adam* awoke from its deep sleep it was astonished. Yahweh brought to *ha-adam* the new creation he had fashioned out of the earth-creature itself. It saw something that was both itself and not itself. What was still one was now two. Adam cried out with the most intense joy. With great delight he sang

> This, finally, is bone of my bone
> And flesh of my flesh
> She shall be called woman.

Darwin did not persuade the Victorian public so convincingly as he did because of the irrefutable logic and evidence of his science. Even his closest scientific supporters did not wholeheartedly accept his thesis, even by the end Darwin himself didn't and, one wonders, of those relatively few people who actually bought and read *The Origin,* how many ploughed through the mass of detailed examples through which Darwin conducts his argument.? Yet by the eighteen-eighties most middle class Victorians, with the exception ironically enough of most of the scientists, had fully accepted evolution by natural selection. Darwin did not convert their intellects, he persuaded their imaginations. In the twentieth century it was seen that Darwin's contribution to the theory of evolution was indeed fully scientific. His identification of the mechanism whereby evolution happens has established him for all time as one of the greatest scientists who has ever lived. The problems that so dismayed the Victorian scientists, the age of the earth and the blending of inherited characteristics, turned out, with the discovery of radiation and the re-discovery of Mendel, not to be problems after all. But this was not the case in the nineteenth century. Of the many ironies, Mendel sent a copy of his paper to Darwin, but he never read it. It remained uncut on his desk. *The Origin* convinced the Victorian public not because it was a great scientific work but because it was a great literary one. What differentiated it from all previous presentations of evolution was that it had the grand style and the magnificently sweeping vision of a creation myth, and they did not. For a creation myth to be acceptable to the nineteenth century it had to give the illusion of scientific credibility. But it was not really the science that compelled. It was the style.

The Origin is full of echoes from the Bible. Like Yahweh Natural Selection is a patient gardener. 'Man selects only for his own good: Nature for the good of the being which she tends'. Despite Darwin's central message of exterminatory meaninglessness, the natural goodness that was Yahweh's purpose in Genesis resounds constantly throughout *The Origin.* Natural selection is 'daily and hourly scrutinizing throughout the world, every variation, even the slightest; rejecting what is bad, preserving and adding up all that is good.' It is always working for 'the good of each being'. 'It will never produce in a being anything injurious to itself, for natural selection acts solely by and for the good of each'. Like Lord God Natural Selection acts within a time frame. But whereas he took a week, Nature adopts far grander chronologies. Whereas God used his time to create, Natural Selection, throwing down the gauntlet boldly, uses hers to exterminate. 'Though nature grants vast periods of time for natural selection, she does not grant an indefinite period….if any one species does not become modified and improved in a corresponding degree with its competitors, it will soon be exterminated.' Especially biblical in its style but unbiblical in its content was Darwin's concluding paragraph. 'Thus, from the war of nature, from famine and death, the most exalted object that we are capable of conceiving, namely, the production of the higher animals, directly follows'. We are back to Marduk. The law of nature itself, the condition of creation, is war. The implicit claim could not be more provocative and more sweeping. The higher animals are not merely the peak of evolution but 'the most exalted object we are capable of conceiving, namely, the production of the higher animals'. Not Yahweh Lord God, whom we once thought was the highest object of which we could conceive, but the higher animals. It did not take eminent Victorians long to work out that the highest of the higher animals were humans, and of those the very highest – a point that *The Descent Of Man* was to reiterate not implicitly but fully explicitly, to their even greater satisfaction – were they themselves. The final appeal is not to Baconianly collated examples, but to the elevation of the soul. The grandeur of Genesis is directly challenged by another, one that deliberately echoes it. 'There is grandeur in this way of life, with its several powers, having been originally breathed into a few forms or into one.' As Yahweh breathed life into *ha-adam,* so evolution has breathed life into an original form. Darwin's 'Light will be thrown…' is irresistibly reminiscent of 'Let there be light'. And as

Genesis begins with the cosmic creation of planets and stars, so *The Origin* ends against a cosmic background, appealing finally not to logic but to wonder. '...and that, whilst this planet has gone cycling on according to the fixed law of gravity; from so simple a beginning endless forms most beautiful and most wonderful have been and are being evolved.'

There are two metaphors that are especially central to *The Origin*. One links it closely to the biblical creation myth out of which it itself evolved and establishes its kinship with it. The second establishes *The Origin* as a new kind of creation myth in its own right, and asserts its claim to have imaginatively destroyed and moved beyond its parent. Darwin's first great central metaphor linking his text with Genesis is that of the Tree of Life. Darwin ends his chapter on Natural Selection thus:

'The affinities of all the beings of the same class have sometimes been represented by a great tree. I believe this simile largely speaks the truth. The green and budding twigs may represent existing; and those produced during each former year may represent the long succession of extinct species. At each period of growth, all the growing twigs have tried to branch out on all sides; and to overtop and kill the surrounding twigs and branches; in the same manner as species and groups of species have tried to overmaster other species in the great battle for life. The limbs divided into great branches; and these into lesser and lesser branches, were themselves once, when the tree was small, budding twigs; and this connection of the former and present buds by ramifying branches may well represent the classification of all extinct and living species in groups subordinate to groups. Of the many twigs that flourished when the tree was a mere bush, only two or three, now grown into great branches, yet survive and bear all the other branches: so with the species which lived during long past geological periods; very few now have living and modified descendants. From the first growth of the tree, many a limb and branch has decayed and dropped off; and these lost branches of various sizes may represent those whole orders, families, and genera which have now no living representatives, and which are known to us only from having been found in a fossil state. As we here and there see a thin straggling branch springing from a fork low down in a tree; and which by some chance has been favoured and is still alive on its summit, so we occasionally see an animal like the Ornithorhincus or Lepidosiren which, in some small degree, connects by its affinities two large branches of life, and which has apparently been saved from fatal competition by having inhabited a protected station. As buds give rise by growth to fresh buds, and these, if vigorous, branch out and overtop on all sides many a feeble branch, so by generation I believe it has been with the great Tree of Life, which fills with its dead and broken branches the crust of the earth, and covers the surface with its ever branching and beautiful ramifications.'

By any standards this is an absolutely superb piece of writing, and surely one of the glories of English prose. The style of the piece enacts what it means. The long sustained single thought, ever gathering momentum through its many ramifications, suggests the long continuing rise of evolution. The metaphorical pattern imitates what it describes, branching out into further and further interconnected similes. 'From the first growth of the tree, many a limb and branch has decayed and dropped off'. How the sentence achieves what it says; springing into a quickening life until it reaches its central climax and then losing its purposefulness in ever lengthening syllables until, in the end, its energy just drops off. The alliterations and balanced cadences and extended clauses are so harmonious that the long paragraph almost achieves the rhythm of poetry. It suggests the majesty and grandeur of the march of life. It turns evolution from a dry scientific theory into the passage of a god. It is a superb piece of pedagogy. It uses an everyday image that the reader is thoroughly familiar with to introduce him to the unfamiliar. Yet it prevents him from compromising the unfamiliarity of Darwin's thought, through an image so familiar that he ceases to wrestle with the argument, by making him look really closely at the metaphor through which the thought is being communicated. Of course, we have all seen thin straggling branches springing from a fork low down on a tree, though that is not a detail usually contained in your everyday working memory of a tree. Just when we are getting perhaps a little over familiar with the imaginative connection being made, Darwin drops in his Ornithorhyncus and Lepidosiren. Finally he makes the connection with Genesis directly. This is not any mere tree, not simply a useful heuristic device. It is the Tree of Life. The gathering energies of the passage, increasingly infusing its thought with emotional life as it proceeds, its driving momentum constantly carrying forward the thrust of the argument, culminates and finally dissipates its dynamism into 'I believe'. Credo. I believe in the Tree of Life.

* * *

But in making this connection the passage also goes beyond it. Darwin claims both fact and metaphor for natural selection. 'I believe this simile largely speaks the truth.' Through this familiar image of a tree, so richly treasured in literature but always suggesting the great rooted blossomer, the fruitful resource, the intermediary between heaven and earth, the high rustling storehouse of peace, Darwin introduces us to his novel thought that this is a terrible battlefield, a theatre of internecine war. The Tree of Life only flourishes because it has covered the crust of the earth with its dead and broken branches. It is because the image is so culturally cherished that Darwin's re-working of it is so devastating. That first suggestion that branches kill each other is a shock. It is because he has drawn us into an imaginative identification with so familiar a friend, because we find that his Trojan horse is already within our gates before we have even thought of erecting our defences, that - much as new species colonize the habitats of old ones and use their resources both to destroy the old and sustain themselves - he is able to use the imaginative power of the profoundest religious symbols to undermine religion. It is perhaps only at an unconscious level that the reader realises that in reading *The Origin Of Species* he is eating of the Tree of Knowledge.

Darwin's other central and immensely suggestive metaphor is that of the hammered wedges. In 1857, in what he called his 'big book' about evolution, that he was in process of laboriously writing when Wallace's essay arrived and catapulted him into concentrating his ideas and thus producing his masterpiece, he had written:

'Nature may be compared to a surface covered with ten thousand wedges; many of the same shape representing different species, all packed closely together and all driven in by incessant blows: the blows being far severer at one time than at another: sometimes a wedge of one form and sometimes of another being struck: the one driven deeply in forcing out others: with the jar and shock often transmitted very far to other wedges in many lines of direction: beneath the surface we may suppose that there lies a hard layer, fluctuating in its level; and which may represent the minimum amount of food required by each living being; and which layer will be impenetrable by the sharpest wedge' [16]

The image was one that would have connected directly with his Victorian audience. England was loud with the noise of actual hammered wedges as canals were dug, railway cuttings were excavated and mines were sunk. But the noise of hammers was also one that connected the expanding industrial revolution with geology and assaults on the literal truth of Genesis. England was full, too, of amateur geologists who were searching diligently for fossils, each hoping to be the one to find the really great treasure that would settle for ever the urgent evolutionary questions that were unsettling the land. 'Those dreadful hammers'. In *The Origin* itself Darwin uses the wedges as a central metaphor for his doctrine that behind the deceptive peace of nature there is a real world of strife, extermination and war. In his chapter on *The Struggle For Existence* he stresses the difficulty we have in realising that behind nature's smiling face there is a horrific theatre of struggle and violence ruled by implacable law. We don't easily see it. 'We behold the face of nature bright

210

with gladness, we often see superabundance of food'. Later in the chapter he connects the two metaphors of the face and the wedges together.

'The face of Nature may be compared to a yielding surface, with ten thousand sharp wedges packed close together and driven inwards by incessant blows, sometimes one wedge being struck and then another with greater force'[17]

The image of a smiling face, innocently bright but now smashed by ten thousand sharp hammered wedges, that maternal face Yahweh Lord God had breathed on so lovingly, is horrific. No image could communicate so graphically the profound convulsion, both expressed and stimulated by Darwin, that was reshaping Victorian England's imaginative understanding of itself. If your intention were to literally assault the face of nature with ten thousand wedges, to shut your ears to the cries of the starving poor, to incarcerate the unwillingly unemployed and the utterly enfeebled in workhouses, and to invade other defenceless countries and exploit their resources, which was indeed the project of Victorian England, then as an imaginative resource and a court of mythic permission Genesis was clearly no longer of use. The Victorians were urgently in need of a new creation myth, and when it came they accepted it with alacrity.

(Endnotes)

1   Desmond and Moore *op. cit.* p.485
2   Himmelfarb *op.cit.* ch. 12
3   Michael Ruse 1975 *The Darwinian Revolution* p. 226. Chicago. Univ Press.
4   Himmelfarb *op.cit.*p.262
5   Robert M. Young *Darwin's Metaphor: Does Nature Select?* Monist 55 (1971) 442-503
6   Ruse *op.cit.* p.238
7   Young *op.cit.*p.478
8   Browne *op.cit.* pp 290-2
9   Ruse *op.cit.* p.240
10 Himmelfarb *op.cit* p.283
11 see Himmelfarb *op.cit.* chs 12-14
12 Janet Browne *op. cit.* chapter 9
13 for what he did say see Himmelfarb *op. cit.* ch. 14
14 Georges Roux 1964. *Ancient Iraq* London Penguin pp. 96-7
15 Phyllis Tribble 1978 *God And The Rhetoric Of Sexuality.* Philadelphia Fortress Press. p 87.
    I am taking most of my ideas and information in this section from Tribble
16 quoted in *Languages Of Nature.* Gillian Beer '*The Face of Nature: The Language of the Origin of Species b*
17 *Origin* p. 119

Chapter 7

The Descent Of Man: From Noble Animals to Ignoble Humans

Many mammalian species solve their problems of aggression through appeasement rituals. Even at the height of a fight when one animal starts to signal that he will give in his opponent immediately becomes his friend. But among primates, with their much more flexible brains, such a powerful instinct operates much less certainly. We therefore find other structures which have developed to achieve the same end. One is the male dominance hierarchy, which is not peculiar to primates but operates amongst them especially importantly.[1] Though these hierarchies may often appear to be very aggressive, their purpose is not to promote aggression but by confirming rank to contain it. Another even more important feature of primate life is the mother-infant bond. Mothers give psychological security to offspring which underlies the relationships of later life. Most importantly they groom their infants, and it is through grooming that adult primates too find security in each other.

In the nineteen-sixties a new generation of female primatologists, including Thelma Rowell, Sara Hrdy, Jane Lancaster and Jane Goodall, began to discover that in most primate societies, despite the ebullience of the male groups, the real core of the social structure is not the male hierarchy based on the prime males, but the matri-focal sub-group based on the old females, who have their own hierarchical ranking. This is because in most primate species it is the males who move out of their natal sub-groups when they become sexually mature and the females who stay, and for this reason become the source of continuity and stability. There are thus two organizational principles found among primates: the one overt, male, hierarchically unstable and founded on power, the other less overt, female, founded on affection between kin, stable, and of much greater underlying importance. In accordance with this there are also two patterns of what have been called attention structures.[2] Among male hierarchies attention is inspired in the subordinate by fear of aggression from the dominant, and is one way only, paid by the subordinate to the dominant,. Chance and

Jolly called this 'agonic'. But in matri-focal sub-groups there is another structure they called 'hedonic'. Here attention is based on affection rather than fear and is reciprocal, given by the superior to the junior as much as vice versa.

Observation of chimpanzees in the wild did not start until the early nineteen-sixties. Even though they were working in quite different parts of Africa, the early researchers - Kortland[3], Albrecht and Dunnett[4], V and F Reynolds[5] and the young Jane Goodall herself when she first went to Gombe - painted a remarkably consistent picture of an almost idyllic way of life.[6] An account of this early research is given by Margaret Power in her book *The Egalitarians: Human and Chimpanzee*. Chimpanzees were happy-go-lucky and strikingly hedonic in their relationships. They were gentle with each other and rarely fought. Solitary feeders, an individual finding a rich source of fruit would call and drum on trees so that others were drawn to the place, and these gatherings sometimes developed into uproarious social events that the Reynolds called 'carnivals'. There were no permanent rulers and leadership was what Margaret Power calls 'charismatic', shifting from animal to animal in accordance with their aptitude in different situations. During Jane Goodall's early years at Gombe the most influential animal was old David Greybeard, even though he was far from being the alpha male. Mothers were extraordinarily affectionate towards their young, who according to Kortland had 'a wonderful life'. Although the males did not know who their own offspring were, they acted together as social fathers and showed great interest in the young, who trusted them absolutely.

In the early nineteen-seventies this picture changed suddenly and drastically. By 1974 Jane Goodall had registered 284 incidents of males fighting, and by 1977 she was observing the rise of the tyrannical male despots at Gombe. [7] Group sexual encounters of males with a female were now often extremely brutal, as was the treatment of infants by males. According to Power, infants at Gombe now show 'anxious clinging' and 'aloof and defiant independence'.[8] In this atmosphere the mothers cannot communicate the security to the infants so essential to primate life. The tyrannical despots were the only role models available to the young males, and they in their turn grew into violent and aggressive adults. Above all, genocide was a newly observed phenomenon of those years. At Gombe the colony split into two parts, and the larger and northern Kasakela group set about the extermination of the southern Kahama section in an extraordinarily brutal and systematic way. When they had picked off their victims one by one, sometimes slowly killing them by slow torture and appearing to relish it, they then took over their territory and breeding females. Exactly the same phenomenon was observed at the same time at the other research centre in Tanzania, the Japanese one at Mahale.

Which of these accounts gives the correct picture of the true nature of chimpanzees? Nearly all primatologists would reply that it is the second (though Frans de Waal, one of the greatest of living primatologists, has consistently argued for the central importance of chimpanzee peace making[9]). They argue that the apparent discrepancy arose simply because the early researchers didn't make enough observations. If they had spent longer studying the chimpanzees they would have discovered how brutal they really are. Chimpanzees are extremely difficult to follow in the wild and for this reason none of the early researchers spent many hours actually observing them. Far more observations have been made since, and these have constantly confirmed infanticide, genocide and violence. It might perhaps seem foolish and arrogant to question the view of most professional primatologists, but I wonder whether on this point they are right. It's true that none of the early researchers spent very long in actual observation, but their accounts are remarkably consistent. If you put them end to end it is an impressive total of research hours. And if, offstage, chimpanzee males had been behaving towards infants as we know they now do, the infants would never have shown the trusting dispositions that Kortland observed. Precisely because aggression and brutality have been observed so frequently since the mid-nineteen-seventies, it becomes incredible that the early observers would have missed all signs of it.

* * *

How then are we to explain this sudden and dramatic deterioration in chimpanzee behaviour? I believe that Power is right in her thesis. Chimpanzee social life is extremely delicately balanced, .and when it comes under intense environmental pressure, as it has done since the nineteen-sixties through ever increasing human encroachment on its habitats, it is highly prone to collapse and replacement by the pathologically and emotionally disturbed rule of males. Because of the damage this causes to the mother-infant relationship it creates an emotional vacuum, and thus becomes endemic and self-perpetuating. Chimpanzees are unlike other primates in that it is not males but females who leave the natal troupes. As a consequence the structure of matri-focal sub-groups, which are so vital to the security of other primates, does not exist among them. Why then did chimpanzee societies not collapse long before the nineteen-sixties? The answer is to be found in affection. Even by primate standards chimpanzee mothers are remarkably affectionate towards their infants. They endow them with such a wealth of emotional security that their offspring can relate to each other quite happily all though their lives, even in the absence of overtly stable social structures. In her early years Jane Goodall observed the affection of chimpanzee mothers towards their young with incredulous wonder. But this makes their societies, and the emotional security on which they are based, exceptionally vulnerable to collapse. When this happens, because there are no maternally based kin-groups, the only "constitutional" form they have is the normally highly implicit male dominance hierarchy, which therefore rapidly becomes the defining structure within which the pathology which is now afflicting them expresses itself.

We share 98.4% of our genes with chimpanzees. We only separated from a common ancestor less than six million years ago. This is why in them we find such an illuminating metaphor for ourselves. What this episode of primate history in Africa reveals to us is how vulnerable amongst the higher primates peaceful and civilized behaviour is, how easily it is unbalanced, and how easily both we and the chimpanzees can revert to more primitive and literally bestial behaviours, appropriate to the life forms from which we both evolved, but perhaps not to chimpanzees and certainly not to humans. There is, however, an important difference between ourselves and the chimpanzees. We have highly developed imaginations whereas they, we must assume, do not. In ourselves the imagination is the clearing house between thought and feeling, between the algorithmic behaviours we have inherited from the animals out of which we evolved and our self-consciousness, between instinct and intention. We imagine actions before we do them, and do them in accordance with the way we have imagined them. This is why mythology, the science of the imagination, is so important. Seeing this is the great revolution Wittgenstein wrought in philosophy. In the *Tractatus Logico-Positivus,* dating from his first phase, he thought that we make pictures of the world through our senses and then try and understand the pictures by talking about them in language. We misunderstand the world, he thought, because we make logical errors in connecting the pictures up through linguistic syntax. But in his later philosophy, in *Philosophical Investigations,* he came to see that it is itself an error to think that our senses give us accurate, sharply defined pictures of the world in the first place. Even before we see the world, the defining stories of the cultures within which we come to consciousness have already distorted the way we see it. We experience the world in the way we have already imagined it, and we imagine it in accordance with the kind of imaginations we have. What shapes our imaginations is not scientific facts but language, above all stories.

Which brings us to *The Descent Of Man.* *The Descent* is far less cogent a scientific work even than *The Origin.* The key facts that it offers as evidence are again and again unverified, merely anecdotal or speculative. But as a myth it is even more powerful. What *The Origin* was to Victorian capitalism, *The Descent* was to imperialism. *The Descent* was the central cult story of the British Empire. It was the major imaginative vehicle through which hedonic values, which had been advocated with such supreme intelligence by Adam Smith, were overthrown by the agonic ones of the male dominance hierarchy and spread round the globe. The beast in man, that violent chimpanzee so deeply encoded in the genes and yet so close to the surface, is held in check by cultures, and cultures assemble themselves round central myths. All over the world, first of all in its western part during the nineteenth century and then in most of the rest of it during the twentieth century, ancient cultures have been destroyed by the advancing industrial revolution, and their core myths usually replaced by one of two new ones, either that of Darwinism or that of Marxism. Both purported to offer irrefutable scientific arguments for their claims, the one drawing its evidence from biology and the other from history. Both promised a much better future for humanity, that would be brought about through the inevitable processes of nature, the one believing that it would come about through natural selection, the other through dialectical materialism. Each was so powerful that it was able to replace religion as the core myth of the societies over which it held sway. But both were fallacious. Both, when taken to the extreme, acted as courts of mythic permission for terrible atrocities, carried out in the name of the superior future societies they promised. It is no accident that as the ancient cultures that had held barbarism in check were destroyed, highly unstable and emotionally disturbed dominance hierarchies, which sometimes included women, practising precisely the brutalities and genocides that primatology would lead us to expect, overtook the twentieth century, just as they had overtaken the Kasakela chimpanzees. Not only did Darwinism and Marxism prove to be cultic myths that were powerless to hold these violent forces in check, while meaning the opposite they positively permitted and enabled them.

Darwin's main intention in *The Descent Of Man* was to show that human beings are just as much the product of the brutally and callously competitive processes of natural selection as any other organic form. He assumes that early human beings progressed, as had all those animal species from which they themselves had developed, as a consequence of warfare between tribes and the extermination of the weak by the strong. But he cannot actually produce any evidence to substantiate this crucial part of his argument, the violently aggressive competition that drove the development of early human beings. All he can produce, as evidence that man too is the product of natural selection and has developed directly out of those animal species that immediately preceded him, is an account of how those behaviours that we associate most specifically with human beings can already be seen operating in other animals. Man's behaviour is only a more fully developed version of theirs. Mankind, it can be seen, arose directly out of them. The logical title that he would better have given his account of the work of natural selection as an explanation for humanity was, perhaps, *The Ascent Of Man.* But just as in *The Origin,* he chose an ambiguous phrase that in at least one of its meanings implied exactly the opposite of what he said he meant. Curiously enough, the comparisons he makes between animal and man in order to further his argument also imply the exact opposite of what he says he means. For he does not give us examples of animals competing with each other, destroying each other and exterminating each other.

On the contrary, he gives us example after example of animals behaving with a grace, generosity and nobility which, under the pen of so great a writer, moves one to tears. Whereas the examples of human behaviour, proposed as evidences of the operation of natural selection in the human species, are often unintentionally characterized by a meanness, cruelty and callousness far more brutal than any that could be found in any brute. A descent indeed. Perhaps Darwin's title spoke more eloquently than he knew. We have little direct evidence of the circumstances under which early man evolved. But it is reasonable to think that the chimpanzees with whom we share nearly all our genes, although they too have evolved, have done so far less than we have, and are therefore much more like the creatures that both primitive chimpanzees and early humans must have been like when both species were still far closer to identity with each other than they are now. Could it be that the hedonic creatures Kortland, Albrecht and Dunnett, the Reynolds and Jane Goodall discovered in the early nineteen-sixties before they had been disturbed by human encroachment and primatological enquiry, are actually the closest we are going to get to a picture of what early humans might actually have been like? And that in both species a descent, from hedonic to agonic, has taken place? But in the human case such falls from grace are always imaginative before they are behavioral. They too have their enabling myths. My proposition is that just as in the Middle Ages men needed to get mythic permission from the Papacy when they wished to act selfishly, cruelly and unnaturally, not in the petty and limited ways that individuals behave badly but on a vast and terrible scale, so in a more irreligious age they needed to get a similar mythic permission from science. *The Descent Of Man* was one of the potent myths, thought this was not what Darwin intended, that enabled the exterminations of whole peoples, the genocides, the morally uninhibited total wars for the survival of genes and the brutal cruelties, that Darwin had only imagined happening amongst primitive early human tribes, but that did happen, in the twentieth century, in actuality.

Darwin's purpose in *The Descent Of Man* is, first and above all, to show that human beings are just as much the consequence of natural selection as any other living form. His second aim is to reconcile the ruthless extermination of the weak that is the method of natural selection with the compassion that is the hallmark of civilized societies. His third aim is to deal with the anxiety that, given the high rate of breeding amongst the inferior classes of society in Victorian England and the habit of late marriage amongst the superior, the benefits of natural selection will be overwhelmed by inferior stock. His final purpose is to explain why, because of natural selection, some races are superior to others. The theoretical procedures of *The Origin,* first the patient accumulation of data, second the observation of regular patterns in the data, and third the deduction of underlying *verae causae* that explain the regularities, are here assumed. As is also the theme of *The Origin,* it is the underlying principles of war, competition and extermination that have led to the progress and improvement of organic forms. Here Darwin is seeking to demonstrate how these principles apply to mankind. His method is to show that all of the higher faculties and behaviours that we associate with man are to be found in embryo in animals, and that just as there is an unbroken continuum of development between lower and higher animals, so there is between the higher animals and man. 'We must also admit that there is a much wider interval in mental powers between one of the lowest fishes, as a lamprey or lancelet, and one of the higher apes, than between an ape and man; yet this interval is filled up with numberless gradations.'[10] The likenesses between animals and man are illustrated with a plentiful supply of examples, often fascinating, diverting and heart-warming.

Darwin first shows that all of the emotions we find in ourselves are also to be found in a less developed form in animals.[11] Animals experience pleasure and pain, happiness and misery. They experience jealousy, fear and rage. The love of a dog for his master is notorious. In the agony of death a dog has been known to caress his master and 'every one has heard of the dog suffering under vivisection, who licked the hand of the operator'. Without doubt animals experience emotions of maternal tenderness. Darwin quotes Whewell: "who that reads the touching instance of maternal affection, related so often of the women of all nations, and of the females of all animals, can doubt that the principle of action is the same in the two cases?". Drawing on his vast fund of data from field correspondents, Darwin notes how Rengger observed an American monkey solicitously driving the flies away from her infant. Duvaucel saw a Hylobates monkey washing the face of her infant in a stream. 'One female baboon had so capacious a heart that she not only adopted young monkeys of other species, but stole young dogs and cats, which she continually carried about.' Animals don't like being laughed at and sometimes invent imaginary offences. In the Zoological Gardens there was a baboon that always got into a furious rage when his keeper took out a book or letter and read it to him. Animals also have a sense of humour; dogs will play practical jokes on their masters by waiting till the last moment before snatching up a stick the master is bending down to retrieve.

Darwin next moves on to the intellectual faculties. Animals experience curiosity. Brehm had told him that monkeys are so curious they will overcome their dread of snakes to the extent of lifting up the lid of a snake box in the zoo and peeping inside before running away in great excitement. Darwin verified the truth of the story for himself by taking a stuffed snake into the monkey house in the Zoological Gardens. Animals also imitate. Wolves brought up by dogs learn to bark, birds learn their songs from their parents, Dureau de la Malle told him of a dog brought up with kittens that learnt to wash itself just like a cat. Animals pay attention, as when a cat intently stalks a bird. They also remember. Sir Andrew Smith wrote to him from the Cape of Good Hope to tell him of a baboon who recognized Sir Andrew with joy after an absence of nine months. Even ants can recognize a fellow member of their own community after a gap of four months. You might think that the imagination is a prerogative of man. But dogs dream and howl at the moon, not looking at the moon, according to his correspondent Houzeau, but at some fixed distant point on the horizon. Moving to the higher faculties, Darwin argues that animals also display rudimentary powers of reason. Houzeau told him how his dogs, suffering from thirst in a desert in Texas, would dig for water in hollows, as if they had worked out that water is most likely to be found in low places. A bear has been observed making eddies in flowing water with his paw, in order to bring a floating piece of bread within his reach. Birds kill themselves by flying against telegraph poles but other birds observe this and learn to avoid them. Darwin himself had seen a young orang who was about to be whipped cover herself with a straw blanket.

Moving on to higher faculties still, Darwin argues that animals practise rudimentary language. They also enjoy a sense of beauty. When a male bird displays gorgeous plumage before a female it is impossible to doubt that he does so because she admires his beauty, and the desire shown by human females to borrow these plumes, so that they too might enhance their beauty in the eyes of the opposite sex, only confirms how alike in this regard humans and animals are. In fact, it might well be thought that some animals have a more highly developed sense of beauty than some humans. 'Judging from the hideous ornaments, and the equally hideous music admired by most savages, it might be argued that their aesthetic faculty was not so highly developed as in certain animals, for instance, as in birds'.[12] Even the religious sense, 'the ennobling belief in the existence of an Omnipotent God' (a phrase put in perhaps to head off criticism from the parsons which in fact never came), can be traced to animal behaviours. There are, it is true, savage tribes who do not practise monotheism or even polytheism. But a belief in 'unseen or spiritual agencies' seems to be universal amongst barbarians. Mr Tylor has shown that such beliefs may have originated in dreams, for 'savages do not readily distinguish between subjective and objective impressions'. When savages dream, the figures they see in the dream are believed to have come from a distance in order to stand over them, or alternatively they believe they have been travelling in far off spiritual realms.

* * *

How the tendency among savages to believe in spiritual essences animating ordinary solid objects may have arisen, was suggested to Darwin by a behaviour he observed one day in his dog. On a hot day a parasol on the lawn was flapping in the slight breeze that was blowing. The dog, who would have made no response if there had been a human being standing near the parasol, started growling. 'He must, I think, have reasoned to himself in a rapid and unconscious manner that movement without any apparent cause indicated the presence of some strange living agent.' Savages naturally attribute to these unknown spiritual agencies the same kind of passions, such as a desire for vengeance, that they themselves feel. York Minster, one of the Fuegians Captain Fitzroy had brought back to England after his first voyage in *The Beagle,* and who was now being brought back to his native land, cried 'Oh Mr Bynoe, much rain, much snow, blow much', a retributive punishment by the spirits, he believed, for wasting food. The feeling of religious devotion is, of course, highly complex and exalted and could only occur in beings of at least moderate intelligence. Nevertheless, we can see the faint beginnings of such high sentiments even in the devotion of a dog to its master. The behaviour when its master returns is quite different to its behaviour towards other dogs. Professor Braubach maintains that the dog looks on its master as a god.

Having established that human emotional and intellectual behaviours have close parallels in the animal realm, Darwin next turns to morality. The moral sense, as Sir James Mackintosh remarks, is the most noble attribute of man. Immanuel Kant exclaims, 'Duty! Wondrous thought, that workest not by fond insinuations, flattery, nor by any threat, but merely by holding up thy naked law in the soul..'.[13] The proto-morality of animals is rooted in their social instincts. They warn each other of danger, groom each other and lick each others' sores. The instinct to join the flock to migrate is so strong that a swallow will even leave her young. Audubon recounts the sad case of a pinioned goose who was so anxious to join his fellows he started out on his long thousand-mile migratory journey on foot. There can be no doubt that social animals feel some kind of love. Brehm recounts an episode in Abysinnia in which big male baboons fought off wild dogs while their troupe passed through a valley. One young male was hopelessly stuck on a rock until one of the largest males, 'a true hero', came back to lead him triumphantly away before the gaze of the amazed dogs. It is true that animals often appear to show no sympathy, as when they expel a wounded animal from the herd or gore it to death. But in this they are no worse than Fijians who bury their old parents alive. And on other occasions, in any case, animals do show sympathy. On a salt lake in Utah Captain Stansbury found an old blind but fat pelican that was being fed by other pelicans. Some years ago in the Zoological Gardens the keeper in the monkey house was attacked by a fierce baboon. A normally timid little American monkey, who was a close friend of the keeper, immediately rushed up and distracted the baboon while the keeper escaped with his life.

This same sympathy is at the root of human behaviour just as it is in animals. Darwin quotes Adam Smith, who put sympathy at the basis of his moral science: "the sight of another person enduring hunger, cold, fatigue, revives in us some recollection of these states which are painful even in idea".[14] Just like the little American monkey, a human being will plunge into a raging torrent to save a drowning man, even though a stranger. Whereas other experiences such as fatigue and hunger pass away when they have been satisfied, the social instinct is with us all the time. It is why we feel remorse and regret when we have failed to live up to the code of the social group in which we find ourselves. Even when we are alone, how often do we think with pleasure and pain of what others think of us? Feelings of guilt seem to have little to do with the content of the moral injunction itself, but with the force of morality as a socially binding code. Hindus feel great guilt if they eat unclean food. Dr Landor told Darwin of an Australian aboriginal who lost his wife to disease, with the consequence that he felt a strong moral obligation to go and spear a woman from another tribe. He insisted on doing so, even though Dr Landor told him he would be imprisoned. There can be no doubt that if, in an extreme case, human beings were brought up like bees, the females would feel a strong obligation to kill the males when their breeding services were over, and mothers would kill their daughters if they found them to be sexual rivals. In primitive societies it can readily be seen that morality is still entirely social. American Indians are honoured if they scalp a member of another tribe. Indian thugs feel guilt if they fail to strangle and kill as many strangers as did their fathers.

In Chapter V Darwin turns directly to the action of natural selection in the development of human societies. The mechanism of advance amongst early humans was that of exterminatory competition. All that we know about savages, he tells us, suggests that in primitive times stronger tribes supplanted weaker ones:

'from the remotest times successful tribes have supplanted other tribes'.[15] An unusually brave or inventive individual arising in a particular tribe would be imitated by his fellows, and this would give them a competitive advantage. It might be thought that the effects of natural selection might be nullified because the bravest would die young and leave no offspring. But moral virtues in individuals only occur in social contexts. An especially brave man would only exist in an especially brave tribe, and it would be the moral superiority of the tribe as a whole which would give it its advantage and survival value. Darwin then turns to the effects of natural selection among civilized nations. 'We civilized men', it is true, do interfere with natural selection by preserving weaklings who would otherwise be eliminated. We build asylums for the insane and workhouses for the feeble, and through vaccination preserve thousands who otherwise would have died from smallpox. On the other hand, although civilization checks in this way the advance of natural selection, it enhances it by means of good food. Civilized men are always found to be far stronger than savages.

An even greater problem is presented by the feckless poor, often degraded by vice, who breed early and prolifically, whereas the careful and frugal marry late and have smaller numbers of children. There is therefore a Malthusian threat that the poor will undo the beneficial action of natural selection altogether. As Mr Greg puts the case: "The careless, squalid, unaspiring Irishman multiplies like rabbits: the frugal, foreseeing, self-respecting, ambitious Scot, stern in his morality, spiritual in his faith, sagacious and disciplined in his intelligence, passes his best years in struggle and in celibacy, marries late and leaves few behind him".[16]

Given a land peopled by a thousand Saxons and a thousand Celts, in a dozen generations five-sixths of the population would be Celts, and five-sixths of the property would belong to the Saxons. In the 'struggle for existence' it would be the less favoured race that had prevailed, not because of its virtues but because of its vices. Darwin's answer to this is that the poor may breed faster but they also die more often. They herd into towns where the death rate is much higher than in the country, especially in the age-bracket one to five. Women who have children when very young die far more often in childbirth, and unmarried feckless ne'er do wells die in far greater numbers than sober married men. This is so much so that Dr Stark has assembled statistics showing that marriage itself is a cause of longevity.

Because of these positive checks on the profligate, the problem is not nearly so great as it might appear. However, it is always a danger and there is no guarantee that any civilized nation will not fall behind. Spain is an example. Partly because the Inquisition killed many of the most intelligent men and partly because others were celibate priests, the Spaniards have become effete. It is a mystery, says Darwin, why the English have 'the daring and persistent energy' which has made them such superior colonists. But we are left in little doubt as to Darwin's solution. 'A nation which produced during a lengthened period the greatest number of highly intellectual, energetic, brave, patriotic and benevolent men, would generally prevail over less favoured nations.'[17] It is natural selection that is responsible for the superiority of the British. It is natural selection too that is responsible for the wonderful progress of the United States, ' for the more energetic, restless, and courageous men from all parts of Europe have emigrated to that great country and have there succeeded best'.

Darwin turns next to race. He has little difficulty in demonstrating that the races are not different species, but all varieties of one single species. Finally he turns to the extinction of races. A remarkable feature of human beings is their ability to live in many different climates and resist many different threats. It is for this reason that each race does not occupy a closely defined niche and why competition for space among humans is so fierce. 'Extinction follows chiefly from the competition of tribe with tribe and race with race.' Various checks are always in action, such as periodic famines, disease, infertility, infanticide and licentiousness, and as soon as one tribe weakens, another will immediately challenge it and 'the contest will soon be settled by 'war, slaughter, cannibalism, slavery and absorption'.[18] When civilized men come into contact with savages the struggle is short, except in cases where disease comes to the aid of the natives. But usually it is the other way round. New diseases prove highly destructive among savages. They cannot or will not adapt new agricultural methods. Spirituous liquors, for which they have so strong a taste, devastate them. They just fade away. Mr Sproat has noted that the natives become "bewildered and dull by the new life around them; they lose the motives for exertion, and get no new ones in their place". The more that natural selection favours a civilized race, the more it favours its further and more and more rapid progress. A few centuries ago Europe feared the inroads of eastern barbarians. Now such an idea would be ridiculous. Mr Bagehot has remarked that formerly savages did not fade away before the onslaught of civilized nations, for there is no lament amongst the classical authors over perishing barbarians.

Now natives just lie down and die before the

240

oncoming Europeans. In Tasmania the population was rated by some as high as 20,000 when the colonists arrived. After 'the famous hunt' by the colonists only 120 were left. In 1832 these were transported to Flinders Island where, in 1835, there were only 100 left. In 1847 they were moved to Oyster Cove by which time only 46 were left. In 1864 there were only one old man and three old women. Their infertility was also remarkable. At Oyster Cove when there were nine women left of child-bearing age, only two had ever conceived. A similar situation pertained among the Maoris in New Zealand, recounted to him by Mr Fenton. A census taken in 1858 showed that their numbers had decreased by 19.42% during the previous fourteen years. The census of 1872 showed that their numbers had dropped further from 53,700 to 36, 359, even though the population was scattered over a wide area and occupied many different habitats. Mr Fenton, again, attributed the fall not primarily to any outside factor but to the infertility of the women. In 1844 there was one non-adult for every 1.57 adults, whereas in 1858 there was one non-adult for every 3.27 adults. An even more devastating story could be told of the Sandwich Islands. When Captain Cook first visited the islands in 1779 the population was estimated to be about 300,000. In 1823 it had dropped to 142,050. In 1832 it was 130,313, in 1853 71,019, by 1872 51, 531. The profligacy of the women, bloody wars, the severe labour imposed by the colonists and disease, all without doubt played a part. But again the chief cause seemed to be the declining fertility of the women. Dr Ruschenberger of the US navy who visited these islands between 1835 and 1837, reported that in one district of Hawaii only 25 men out of 1134, and in another only 10 out 637, had as many as three children. Of eighty married women only 39 had ever borne children. The official report only gave an average of half a child to each married couple on the island.

Thus Darwin lays the blame for the extinction of races fairly and squarely on nature. Natural causes of infertility such as malaria or inbreeding can be discounted. A far more suggestive analogy, he thinks, is that between primitive human beings and animals. Wild animals that have been transplanted or taken into zoos often fail to breed. Elephants moved from Java to India ceased to have young. Monkeys kept in zoos where theoretically the conditions for rearing young should have been much more favourable

likewise became sterile. The susceptibility of fertility to changed conditions among primitive peoples and animals contrasts vividly with the situation among civilized peoples, where just the opposite seems to apply. The population of Pitcairn soared after the English arrived and started breeding with native women. The problem is exactly the same as that of the fossil horse which rapidly disappeared from South America after the appearance of the Spanish horse. The natives too seem to know this. The New Zealander compares his fate with that of the native rat, now almost completely exterminated by the European rat. 'Though the difficulty is great to our imagination, and really great, if we wish to ascertain the precise causes and their manner of action, it ought not to be so to our reason, as long as we keep steadily in mind that the increase of each species and each race is constantly checked in various ways; so that if any new check, even a slight one, be super-added, the race will surely decrease in number; and decreasing numbers will sooner or later lead to extinction; the end, in most cases, being promptly determined by the inroads of conquering tribes.' [19]

In much of this Darwin was simply imposing

the prejudices of himself and his age on mankind's evolutionary past. How did Darwin know that 'the ennobling religious sense', an experience of which he in his later life seems to have been so singularly lacking, first came about through savages attributing an inner life to accidentally moving material objects, just as his dog did? Why should it not have come about because savages naturally feel an overwhelming sense of numinous awe in the presence of nature, that only unusual poets such as Wordsworth or G.M. Hopkins have expressed among civilized peoples? A book like *Touch The Earth,* a collection of Native American accounts of religious experiences of nature[20], would suggest that this is far more likely to have been the case. Virtually all primitive religious beliefs are far more sophisticated and complex than Darwin's account would suggest. How did he know that primitive people, already wracked by disease and want, lived in a constant state of competitive war and aggression? Napoleon Chagnon has famously described just such a state of affairs amongst the primitive Yananamo in Brazil. But later anthropologists have suggested, though not necessarily correctly, that the astute natives put on displays of aggression especially to gain Chagnon's approval, much as Derek Freeman showed

244

that the Samoans provided Margaret Mead with fabricated evidence to sustain her thesis that they lived in a guilt-free sexual paradise.[21] Anthropologists like Clive Gamble, for example, have painted a completely different picture to Chagnon's. In hunter-gatherer situations, where humans are generally few and the hazards of life great, tribes survive by maintaining very close alliances with each other. If your water-hole might fail at any time, then it is best to have reciprocal rights in somebody else's.[22] Such alliances are sealed and maintained by the exchange of gifts and the exchange of women. Far from primitive peoples being constantly assailed by rampant disease, studies suggest that hunter-gatherers tend to be healthier than dwellers in agrarian and urban societies. They also live a more spacious life with more free time than advanced peoples. Primitive cave art, of which Darwin knew nothing, suggests high degrees of skill and sophistication and gives us no evidence of the endemic aggressive competition Darwin assumed.

Could it be that there has indeed been a descent of man? But it is not the ascent to the high evolutionary peak of Victorian England that Darwin took for granted. Nobody now would believe in the myth of the noble savage. But could it be, comparatively at any rate, that primitive mankind lived in the hedonic happy-go-lucky condition that the early researchers discovered still existing among the chimpanzees in the nineteen-sixties, a picture into which Darwin's heart-warming account of noble and heroic behaviour in animals fits well, and from which we have descended only by degrees to the oppressions, exploitations and cruelties of more recent times?   Could it be that in primitive eras mankind's struggle to survive was so all-absorbing it bred into human beings a tender solicitude for each other, and a dependency on each other, that has become our truly native condition?   Where is the evidence that early human beings lived in a constant state of aggression, competition and war? There is no more evidence than there is that animals and plants do.

* * *

Darwin's own discovery that all mankind are descended from a common stock, within a tiny fraction of time in evolutionary terms, and his own observations that amongst animals sympathy can even cross species boundaries, as in the case of the female baboon with the capacious heart, suggest that it is far more likely

246

that humans naturally feel kinship with each other before they feel hostility. Different families and different races may have slightly different versions of the human genome. Darwinian biology has tended to obscure the profounder fact that these are, after all, only slightly different versions of the same genes. The example of the Kasakela chimpanzees teaches us how easily primates degenerate from loving and peaceable creatures, of which Darwin gives us so many beautiful examples in *The Descent,* into selfish and aggressive competitors and exterminators. It is all too obvious that human beings are not exempt from this general rule. But human beings need courts of mythic permission to sanction these descents. It is perhaps ironic that, in an age when declining religion was increasingly unable to fulfil this function that it had performed so ignobly and for so long, it was the noble and gentle Darwin who supplied the mythic permission that was required.

(Endnotes)

1   See Thelma Rowell 1974. The Concept of Dominance
    Behavioral Biol. (11):131-154
2   See Chance MRA 1967: Attention Structures as the basis
    of Primate Rank Orders. Man (2): 503-518. Also Chance
    MRA & Jolly CJ 1970. Social Groups Of Monkeys,
    Apes and Men. London. Cape.
3   A. Kortland 1962. 'Chimpanzees in the Wild' *Scientific*

American 206 (5): 138-148

4   H., Albrecht & S.S. Dunnett (1971) *Chimpanzees in Western Africa* Munich, Piper

5   V. & F. Reynolds 1965 'Chimpanzees of the Budongo Forest' in *Primate Behavior* ed. I. De Vore pp. 368-424 New York. Holt, Rinehart & Winston.

6   Margaret Power 1991. The Egalitarians: Human And Chimpanzee. Cambridge. CUP

7   See Jane Goodall 1986. The Chimpanzees of Gombe. Cambridge Mass. Harvard Univ. Press & 1990. Through a Window. London. Weidenfeld & Nicholson

8   See Power pp. 88-95

9   See de Waal F.B.M. 1982. Chimpanzee Politics: Power And Sex among Apes. London. Jonathan Cape. Also 1989. Peacemaking among the Primates. Cambridge Mass. Harvard U.P. Also with Jessica C. Flack 2000. Any animal Whatever: Darwinian Building Blocks of Morality In Monkeys And Apes. *In* Evolutionary Origins Of Morality ed. Leonard D. Katz. Exeter Uk. Imprint Academic

10   C. Darwin 1874 *The Descent Of Man* ed. 1998 Prometheus Books New York

11   *Descent* ch 3

12   *op. cit.* p. 96

13   Quoted on p.100 of *The Descent* by Darwin from Kant's *Metaphysics Of Ethics* trans. J.W. Semple 1836

14   Adam Smith *Theory of Moral Sentiments*

15   *Descent* p. 133

16   ibid p.143

17   ibid pp. 146-151

18   ibid. pp189-199

19   ibid. p.199

20   *Touch The Earth* compiled by T.C. McLuhan. 1972. London Abacus

21   These accusation were made in a 1964 book by Patrick Tierney called *Darkness in el Dorado* but were fiercely rebutted by Chagnon.

22   Gamble C. 1982. *Interaction And Alliance In Paleolithic Society,* Man (17) 92-107

Chapter 8
A Slow Dying Amongst Barnacles

The tragedy of Darwinism lies in the confusion in its originator's mind between facts and their meanings. The facts that Darwin discovered are amongst the most important in the whole realm of science. The meanings he assigned to them, everything that he meant by Natural Selection in fact, were misleading and fallacious. In the 1830s, the decade during which Darwin returned home from his famous voyage and conceived his great idea, there was still a struggle going on for the soul of England between sublimity of feeling, which had reached its most self-conscious and forceful expression in the works of the romantic poets, and the rationalism that was being put forward by Bentham and the Utilitarians. By 1859, when Darwin published *The Origin,* Benthamism was totally in the ascendent. Utilitarianism had become the central principle of English public life, and the great cosmic visions of the romantic poets were fast degenerating into the sentimentalities of the mid-Victorians. Between the conception and birth of *The Origin*, this triumph of rationalism entered deeply into Darwin and damaged him profoundly. It was not simply that he put a false interpretation on what he had discovered. More tragically still, his narrowing vision, acute personal loss and dessicating sensibility led him to miss other precious meanings that are implicit in his great discovery. Through his works, unfortunately, he went on to inflict the deep damage that he had sustained within himself upon the whole world. If he had understood his discovery differently, and had communicated that different vision to the Victorian public, how differently might they have seen their empire, and what a difference that might have made to subsequent history.

Charles Darwin must have been by nature one of the dearest men who ever breathed. He was modest, humble, gentle, exquisitely sensitive and extraordinarily compassionate, even to the lowliest of creatures. He was profoundly disturbed by the sufferings of sub-human life, by the caterpillar whose body is eaten away from within by the larva of the ichneumon fly, even by a cat playing with a mouse. This extremely self-effacing man once stopped his carriage, got down and assaulted a complete stranger whom he saw maltreating a horse. He had a most noble love of truth and justice. Outraged by slavery, it was the one subject over which he nearly came to blows with Captain Fitzroy on *The Beagle*. 'The remembrance', his son wrote, 'of screams or other sounds heard in Brazil, when he was powerless to interfere with what he believed was the torture of a slave, haunted him for years, especially at night.' [1]   Meeting in Brazil a charming Irishman called Patrick Lennon and, very taken with him, returning with him to his plantation, he was appalled to see Lennon turning into a hideous monster when dealing with his slaves. Lennon would take all the slave women and children from their menfolk and sell them at the market in Rio, even a little mulatto he had fathered himself. 'Picture to yourself', wrote Darwin in anguish, 'the chance, ever hanging over you, of your wife and your little children – those objects which nature urges even the slave to call his own – torn from you and sold like beasts to the first bidder!' [2] He was himself the most loving of parents. On the only occasion when he was known to have spoken a cross word to one of his children, once when his son Francis appeared to be apologizing for the brutal behaviour of the infamous Governor Eyre in Jamaica, he was unable to sleep all night and could not rest until he had begged his son's forgiveness in the morning.

His anguished suffering when his beloved daughter Annie died is almost beyond description. He could make no sense of the cruel death of his nine-year-old daughter. His was the classic case of the appalled human who cannot accept that a loving and merciful God could allow such terrible and senseless things to happen. Ironically, his grief was compounded by guilt that he had handed on to Annie what we would now call a genetic disposition, or an inherited variation as he would have said, which expressed itself in the mysterious wasted condition that laid him low for months on end and took her life. She was, he feared, a victim of natural selection. Becoming increasingly desperate as her malady worsened, he took her to Malvern to be treated by Dr Gully, the hydrotherapist who had ministered to his own condition. At Edinburgh he had given up medicine because he could not bear to be at the bedside of a tortured child. Now the child was his own. At Malvern he watched at her bedside night and day and broke down completely. She rallied, and he was 'foolish with delight'. But there was no recovery. He wept and wept. How gladly he would have sacrificed his own life if only she could live. But Annie sank lower and lower until finally she died. Annie, he wrote later '..was all but perfect....generous and handsome and unsuspicious, free from envy and jealousy, good-tempered and never passionate'. He had never had to reprimand her. 'A single glance of my eye, not of displeasure (for I thank God I hardly ever cast one on her) but of want of sympathy would for some minutes alter her whole countenance'. It was this fine sensitivity that left her 'crying bitterly ...on parting with Emma even for the shortest interval', and that made her exclaim when she was very young, "Oh Mamma what should we do if you were to die". She had very physically affectionate ways, and from earliest infancy would fondle her parents, much to their delight. 'All her habits were influenced by her loving disposition'. After her death Charles cried for days and days and never got over it.[3]

As a young man Darwin was full of fire and passion. He read the poets - Gray, Shelley, Keats, Byron, Wordsworth, Coleridge and most especially Milton -

with great enjoyment. Music and painting gave him extreme pleasure. He deeply loved Handel's *Messiah,* and the anthems during evensong that he had heard in King's Chapel while an undergraduate made him 'shiver with delight'.[4] When twenty-nine, he spoke of getting up close to a painting and being laid open by 'the peculiar smell', presumably varnish, to the 'old irrational ideas' that 'thrilled across me' in his early twenties in the Fitzwilliam Museum in Cambridge.[5] Above all he was deeply moved to ecstasy by natural scenery. Standing upon the summit of the Andes and gazing at the prospect all around he felt 'as if his nerves had become fiddle strings and had all taken to rapidly vibrating'. [6] In Patagonia 'the stillness and desolation' gave him inexplicable pleasure.[7]

* * *

On top of the Andes:

'The atmosphere so resplendently clear, the sky an intense blue, the profound valleys, the wild broken forms, the heaps of ruins piled up during the ages, the bright coloured rocks, contrasted with the quiet mountains of Snow, together produced a scene I could never have imagined.......I felt glad I was by myself, it was like watching a thunderstorm, or hearing a chorus of *The Messiah* in full orchestra'. [8]

* * *

In the Cape Verde Islands:

'here I first saw the glory of tropical vegetation. Tamarinds, Bananas & Palms were flourishing at my feet – I had expected a good deal, for I had read Humboldt's descriptions & I was afraid of disappointments: how utterly vain such fear is, none can tell but those who have experienced what I today have. – It is not only the gracefulness of their forms or the novel richness of their colours, it is the numberless & confusing associations that rush together on the mind, and produce the effect. – I returned to the shore treading on volcanic rocks, hearing the notes of unknown birds, & seeing new insects fluttering about still newer flowers. – It has been for me a glorious day, like giving to a blind man eyes – he is overwhelmed with what he sees and cannot justly comprehend it - Such are my feelings and such may they remain – '[9]

* * *

In the Guyatecas

'It was fortunate we reached this shelter. For now a real storm of T. del Fuego is raging with its wonted fury. White massive clouds were piled up against a dark blue sky & across them black ragged sheets of vapor were rapidly driven. The successive ranges of mountains appeared like dim shadows: it was a most ominous sublime scene. – The setting sun cast on the woodland a yellow gleam much like the flame of spirits of wine on a man's countenance'[10]

* * *

While journeying to Rio

'At night in these fine regions of the Tropics there is one sure & never failing source of enjoyment; it is admiring the constellations in the heaven. – Many of those who have seen both hemispheres give the victory to the stars of the North. – It is however to me an inexpressible pleasure to behold those constellations, the first sight of which Humboldt describes with such pleasure…'[11]

* * *

In Rio de Janeiro

'At this elevation the landscape has attained its most brilliant tint.- I do not know what epithet such scenery deserves: beautiful is much too tame; every form, every colour is such a complete exaggeration of what one has ever beheld before.- If it may be so compared, it is like one of the gayest scenes in the Opera House or Theatre'[12]

* * *

In Terra Del Fuego

'The gloomy depth of the ravines well accorded with the universal signs of violence.- in every direction were irregular masses of rock & uptorn trees, others decayed and others ready to fall. – to have made the scene perfect there ought to have been a group of Banditti – in place of it a seaman (who accompanied me) & myself, being armed and roughly dressed were in tolerable unison with the surrounding Magnificence'[13]

* * *

Again in Terra Del Fuego

'In many places magnificent glaciers extended from the mountains to the water's edge. – I cannot imagine anything more beautiful than the beryl blue of these glaciers, especially when contrasted with the Snow'[14]

* * *

But above all it was in the great Brazilian rainforests that he felt most keenly the sense of the sublime, in 'the great, wild, untidy, luxuriant hothouse' of the Amazon.[15] In Brazil even Humboldt's 'glorious descriptions' did not do justice to the reality. Darwin was dazed by:

"the luxuriance of the vegetation... the elegance of the grasses, the novelty of the parasitical plants, the beauty of the flowers' His mind was 'a chaos of delight'. Pausing in a shady nook, he listened to the droning, croaking, throbbing life. Now, as in ages past, when no human interlopers were around to hear, the forest reverberated to ' a most paradoxical mixture of sound and silence', like some great cathedral at evensong, with the anthem fading to 'universal stillness'. Adding 'raptures to...raptures' he began collecting flowers enough to 'make a florist go wild', and countless beetles. Such 'transports of pleasure' he had never known".[16]

'The air is motionless and has a peculiar chilling dampness. – While sitting on the trunk of a decaying tree amidst such scenes , one feels an inexpressible delight. – The rippling of some little brook, the tap of a Woodpecker, or scream of some more distant bird, by the distinctness with which it is heard, brings a conviction of how still the rest of Nature is...'[17]

'Again I went to the forest which has proved so fruitful in all kinds of animals. – It is probably the last time that I shall ever wander in a Brazilian forest – I find the pleasure of such scenes increases instead, as might have been expected, diminishing ...'[18]

It was beyond description, a source of incommunicable delight, more marvellous, in his own comparison, than the landscapes of Claude Lorraine. Several times during the voyage he felt totally transported by an experiential influx of the sublime, invaded by 'the higher feelings of wonder, admiration and devotion' that, he felt at the time, bore irresistible testimony to God and the immortality of the soul.[19]

*   *   *

By the time he published *The Origin* this wonderful man was already beginning to die within. In his *Autobiography* he lamented the death of his aesthetic sense.

'Formerly, pictures gave me considerable, and music very great delight. But for many years now I cannot endure a line of poetry; I have tried lately to read Shakespeare, and found it so intolerably dull that it nauseated me... My mind seems to have become a kind of machine for grinding general laws out of a large collection of facts, but why this should have caused the atrophy of that part of the brain alone, on which the higher tastes depend I cannot conceive'.[20]

His inability to feel aesthetic delight was deeply bound up with his increasing distaste for religion. The sublime, which he had experienced so powerfully during *The Beagle* voyage, had formerly induced in him strong feelings of devotion, awe and reverence. 'Great art', writes Donald Fleming of Darwin, 'by association with scenic grandeur, scenic grandeur with religion, and all three with the sublime, became part of a single universe of experience'[21] And in his autobiography Darwin himself attests to the connection between scenic grandeur and religion. 'The state of mind which grand scenes formerly excited in me, and which was intimately connected with a belief in God, did not essentially differ from that which is often called the sense of sublimity'. Grand natural scenes, which he had felt so acutely as a young man, arouse 'the powerful though vague and similar feelings aroused by music… which readily pass into devotion'. [22] But now grand scenery 'does not cause me the exquisite delight which formerly it did'[23] His old delight in pictures and music had likewise deserted him: 'Music generally sets me thinking too energetically on what I have been at work on , instead of giving me pleasure.'[24] Worst of all, even his power to feel deep love for his friends had deserted him: 'Whilst I was young and strong I was capable of very warm attachments, but of late years, though I still have very friendly feelings towards many persons, I have lost the power of becoming deeply attached to anyone, not even so deeply to my good and dear friends Huxley and Hooker, as I should formerly have been.'[25]

* * *

He came to feel that scenic grandeur, art, religion and music all colluded in arousing irrational passions in man that clouded his reason. Increasingly he accepted Bentham's dictum that all art is lies. In *The Descent Of Man* he lumped together the gusts of emotion that whip through a crowd of African Negroes, the chattering of monkeys and 'the sensations and ideas' aroused by music in modern man that are 'from their vagueness yet depth, like mental reversions to the emotions and thoughts of a long-past age'[26]. Art alluringly tells us lies by clouding our reason. It gives us no true evidence of anything, but instead substitutes irrational emotions that by right belong to a human past long since overtaken by natural selection. In being seduced by the arts the most advanced products of evolution, the eminent Victorians themselves, were not being faithful to the truths of science. Music 'arouses dormant sentiments of which we had not conceived the possibility, and do not know the meaning; or, as Richter says, tells us of things we have not seen and shall not see'. Finding Shakespeare intolerably dull, music leaden on the ear, scenic grandeur not what it had been and even friendship unsatisfying, Darwin fell back on having his wife read trite and sentimental Victorian novels. Even the impeccably free-thinking

George Eliot was rejected for writing novels that were too serious and emotionally disturbing. Of these cheap and sentimental novels 'A surprising number have been read aloud to me, and I like all if moderately good, and if they do not end unhappily – against which a law ought to be passed. A Novel, according to my taste, does not come into the first class unless it contains some person whom one can thoroughly love, and if it be a pretty woman all the better'. [27]

The bleak vision that conceived the rich and gorgeous varieties of life as the products of war, famine, pestilence, extermination and death was surely not unconnected with this terrible internal dying. More tragically still, it blinded Darwin to the great truths that were implicit in his wonderful discovery: the unity of all life, the developing beauty of organic forms, and the increasingly complex inwardness that is the characteristic hallmark of living things.

––––––––––––––––––––––

(Endnotes)

1   *Life and Letters of Charles Darwin* III 200
2   Browne *op. cit.* Vol 1 pp213-214

3   Desmond and Moore *op. cit.* ch 25

4   Donald Fleming *Charles Darwin: The Anaesthetic
    Man* Victorian Studies 4. (1961) pp. 219-36

5   *ibid*

6   *Life and Letters* III 54

7   Desmond and Moore *Darwin* London Penguin 1992. p.145

8   *Voyage of The Beagle* p. 394

9   Browne *op.cit.* p.164

10 Charles Darwin's *Beagle Diary* ed. R.D. Keynes
    1988 p.273

11 *Beagle Diary p.48*

12 xii *Beagle Diary*

13 *Beagle Diary* 125

14 *Beagle Diary* p. 139

15 *C. Darwin. Journal Of Researches Into The Geology
    And Natural History Of Various Countries
    Visited by H.M.S. Beagle* 1839. pp590, 604

16 Desmond and Moore *op.cit.* p.119

17 *Beagle Diary* p.74

18 *Beagle diary* p.76

19 *Autobiography,* p.91

20 Browne *op. cit.* p. 429

21 Fleming *op.cit.* p. 226

22 *Autobiography* pp. 91-92

23 *ibid.* p.138

24 *ibid.* p. 138

25 *ibid.* p. 115

26 *Descent* p.336

27 *Autobiography* po. 138

Chapter 9
The Origin That Might Have Been

My proposition is that Darwin misinterpreted the facts he had discovered largely because of the constrictions of his religious and philosophical background. Was there another philosophy available to him that, if circumstances had been different, might have led him to a quite different understanding of descent with modification? Yes, there was. It was that of Kant, who, if he had been as well known to Darwin as Locke was, would have introduced him to a quite other thought world. Most importantly, Kant's teaching on teleology in nature was by no means incompatible with what Darwin had discovered about the origin of species, whereas Paley's, the only version of teleology that Darwin knew, was. If Darwin had been soaked in Kantian ideas, he might well have seen that a natural origin was not only compatible with religious belief, but a wonderful enrichment of it. Because Darwin had no understanding of the Kantian background to Humboldt's thinking, the influence Humboldt had on him was almost entirely on his feeling life, and hardly at all on his ideas. The result was that when he came to write *The Origin* and put into intellectual order the insights he had first had on *The Beagle,* twenty years after the epic voyage, there was no way in which he could integrate the Humboldtian element that then had influenced him so much, either into his mind or his text. This is the great tragedy of *The Origin,* for, on the voyage, everything he thought and felt occurred within the aura of ecstatic wonder to which Humboldt had introduced him. On the voyage, everything was related to form and the beauty of form. Twenty years later he had no interest in either form or beauty. What was it that Kant and Humboldt taught, that might have wrought such great changes in Darwin's world view, if he had only understood them as well as he understood Locke and Malthus?

In 1851 Annie died. It concentrated his growing pessimism into a kind of poison. The world of glory he had discovered in South America shrank to the small circle of light beneath his microscope as he grimly and remorselessly studied the barnacles. Most important of all, perhaps, he became a sad man, and it was for this reason that he wrote a sad book. The sublimity that 'as formerly it had done' had so ravished him, had now become meaningless. He was no longer moved by friendship, scenery and music. When he confronted his past it was almost as if he was trying to enter into the feelings of another person whose experiences he did not understand. In a profound sense, astonishing as it may seem, he deeply forgot about the great excursive journey that had revealed so much to him. In the end he fell back, behind and before the voyage of *The Beagle,* on to his Whig upbringing and the ideas of Locke and Paley that had been his first formative influences. In the end, as in the beginning, he was a Whig and it was for this reason that he wrote a Whiggish book. But what a different book he might have written if Kant had entered into his bones and his brain as deeply as Locke did. Only in the very last sentence of *The Origin* - 'There is grandeur in this view of life…' – do we get a scrap of suggestion of the Humboldtian work that might have been.

* * *

1. Kant

Immanuel Kant was Professor of Logic and Metaphysics at the University of Konigsberg in

Prussia. At the beginning of his academic life, he was a conventional enough follower of the rationalism of Leibniz and Wolff that dominated philosophical thinking on the Continent at the time. According to this school, we can only discover the laws of science by logical deduction. There may happen or not happen to be two stones in one part of your garden and two in another. But it is also the case that if you put them together you will inevitably have four. There are therefore inexorable laws of logic working in nature just as there are in the mind, and we discover them by deducing more complex laws from simpler ones. Kant, who was himself partly Scottish, was 'awoken from his dogmatic slumbers', as he put it, by reading David Hume's *An Enquiry Concerning the Human Understanding* and *A Treatise Concerning Human Nature.* Hume agreed that within the mind there are absolutely certain and irrefutable logical truths. Two and two are always going to be four. But we do not actually see the principles underlying science, such as causality, working in nature. What we see are sequential series of events in which, for example, the action of the cue is followed by the rolling of the billiard ball – Hume was a great player of billiards and backgammon so he must have seen a lot of cues striking balls – but we don't actually *see* causality. How, then, can we be certain that it exists? Usually dawn is caused by the sun rising above the horizon. Can we be absolutely certain, in the way that we are certain that two and two make four, that it is going to happen tomorrow? Kant couldn't find an answer to this. Now he started thinking about it, he realized that the rationalist position was itself highly illogical and contradictory. Deductively you can prove both that space must have a boundary, but also that it cannot have a boundary; both that the world must have had a beginning and also that it could not have had a beginning.

But Kant wasn't satisfied by Hume's scepticism either. Newton's laws are deductively and unassailably true, and have been shown by many experiments to be out there actively present and working in nature. The critical case for Kant was geometry. No amount of looking at actual material triangles will tell you that the three angles in the corners add up to two right angles, still less to a straight line. If you just had a pile of triangles that you were trying to fit together, how do you know that you might not find three that when fitted together added up to more than a straight line? But *we do know* that there is no possibility that one day we might come across a triangle that adds up to 181 degrees. Yet there is no law of one hundred and eighty degreeness for triangles empirically discernible in nature, just as we never actually see a law of causality. You might, perhaps, just about be able to imagine that one day all the atoms in a cue and a billiard ball might happen to line up in such a way that the ball didn't roll across the baize but flew up into the air. Or you might even conceive of the possibility of a huge asteroid entering the solar system and knocking the earth out of its orbit so that the sun didn't rise tomorrow. But you can't even imagine the three angles of a triangle adding up to 181 degrees, because you are absolutely certain that they could not. Yet could there be some non-Euclidean geometry somewhere in which this was the case? After all, we now know about geometries that can measure angles on curved surfaces. Or if a sub-atomic entity can so defy logic as to be, at the same time, both an invisible wave moving across the universe and a physical particle occupying a minute point in space, and revealing itself as one or the other in accordance with the question the investigator asks, then what illogicality might not be possible? Could there be other universes in which the most elementary laws of logic that we take for granted do not hold? How do we know that the scientific deductions we make actually describe the reality in this one?

* * *

How can we solve this conundrum? Kant reasoned that just as when we experience colour we don't actually see longer and shorter light waves but see red and green, because our minds have translated physical sensations into psychological categories, so it must be with all our experiences of nature. What we experience when we view nature is not nature itself but our own experiences of it. We know it through the filter of our minds. And because our minds work in terms of unassailably true logical relations, we can only experience nature in accordance with them. Thus we impose our own way of knowing space and time, for example, on nature, and in our way of knowing space the three angles of a triangle have to add up to 180 degrees. But we have no way of knowing what it is that corresponds to space and time in nature itself would be like, if we could know it in some other way than through our minds. Newton's laws are not about nature exactly, but about nature as known by us. We

271

start with experiences of red and eventually deduce that they must have been caused by light waves. But suppose our starting point had been different. There are rare people, after all, who experience colours not as things seen but as things touched. Suppose we normally saw colours as people are said to do when on LSD, not as a single aspect of a thing but as somehow, indescribably, multi-dimensional. How different our science of optics might then be. When we know a thing we have no way of knowing what the thing in itself, the supersensible or the *ding an sich* as Kant called it, is really like, but only the thing as we know it.

Many people think of Kant's *Critique Of Pure Reason* as his definitive work and his other two *Critiques,* the *Critique of Practical Reason* and the *Critique Of Judgment,* as minor addenda. This is a capital error. The three works belong indissolubly to each other, and if Kant had stopped at the first he would in practice be offering a philosophy only marginally less sceptical than Hume's. Kant's crucial teaching in the two later critiques is that in the practical, as opposed to the purely theoretical sides of life, *we do* have some direct knowledge of the *ding an sich.* The theme of Kant's second treatise is moral obligation. He calls this practical reason because we actually have to decide whether or not we are going to steal that purse or perform that particular act of kindness. You can get by in life without worrying about whether red is out there or not. You can't get by without considering how you are going to live. Leibniz and the rationalists taught that since we can show by reason that we are living in a perfect world, then we can deduce that we too are meant to behave perfectly, hence our sense of moral obligation. Kant's objection to this is that since we ourselves are part of the world, but imperfect, the world itself therefore can't be perfect. Hume, on the other hand, thought that all morality is just convention. It pays to be truthful to other people because if everybody tells the truth it is a considerable convenience when doing business or playing backgammon. Kant's objection here is that this simply isn't the way we experience moral obligation. We experience it as absolutely and universally binding. I don't say that I shouldn't tell lies because I am living in the UK, but of course if we were in Korea that would be different.

I am not part of a committee, chaired by David Hume, that has decided that on the whole honesty is the best policy because it pays. Nor do I decide for myself that telling lies is wrong, I simply awake to find myself already living under an imperative obligation. Nor do moral commands apply in some circumstances but not in others. They are categorical, even if they cause me considerable inconvenience, even great suffering, and in abrogating them I would harm no-one else. I do not work out the moral law by observing nature, as I might work out Newton's laws of motion. In acknowledging the moral law I realise I am independent of nature. Nor do I only know the moral law indirectly through the filter of my mind. I know it directly because it is already in my mind. Striving to be virtuous also causes me intense happiness in a quite other sense than seeking greater physical comfort might. The moral law within and the starry sky above are great wonders that assure me of my identity as a transcendental being. In the *Critique Of Practical Reason* I have a direct, though limited, knowledge of the universality and transcendence of the supersensible, the *ding an sich,* which has not come to me through studying nature, the very thing that was denied to me in the first *Critique.* There are other aspects of it, though, which I do not know certainly and directly but which it is reasonable to deduce. If I feel within me an obligation to become ultimately entirely virtuous, what Kant calls the Final Cause, then clearly this is hardly possible in this present world, so it is reasonable to think that I must be an immortal soul. Since I can find no cause for my sense of universal moral obligation in nature, it is reasonable to think that its cause must be God, but of these concepts I have no direct intuition or absolute certainty. What I do know directly is the universality and transcendence that is the true arena of my moral nature.

Kant goes even further in claiming a direct knowledge of the supersensible, and so completing his trilogy, in the *Critique of Judgment.* The question with which he starts here is that of aesthetic judgment, a phrase which seems to contradict itself. 'Aesthetic' implies a purely subjective personal feeling, while 'judgment' implies a statement of objective truth. Is it the case that Bach's music is objectively beautiful and always will be, even though a few people don't think so - though all true music lovers think they are wrong of course - or is it just that it pleases me? Can I *prove* that they are wrong? In giving his answer, Kant argues that the contradiction is resolved because the beautiful brings us directly into contact with the supersensible.

Although my only evidence that something is beautiful is my own personal feeling that it is, the beauty that I feel is beauty itself. As usual in his philosophy, Kant is reacting both against the continental rationalists and the British empiricists. Hume denied that beauty is an objective quality of things; according to him it is a wholly subjective feeling aroused in the beholder by a particular arrangement of appearances in the object. In the same sort of way that a pebble you brought back from your holiday has none of the pleasure of the holiday actually in it, but arouses pleasure in you because you associate it with long and happy sunny days, so all beautiful objects are pleasing because they stimulate pleasurable associations in the beholder. Complexes of pleasurable associations experienced by persons of refined discernment and taste over the ages coalesce into general standards of beauty, and it is these that we learn and then apply when we gain pleasure from beautiful things. Burke too thought that beauty is not in any way actually in objects, but only in our ideas of them. He goes beyond Hume in that he not only analyses the beautiful but the sublime. His account is purely psychological; sublimity is in no way actually in the objects. We simply *call* things sublime if they evoke in us feelings of awe mixed with a kind of fear and horror.

Kant was at war with these ideas just about as much as it is possible to be. In his view they described exactly what an experience of beauty is not. The whole point is that it is personal and unmediated. Truths of science I can learn at second hand. I can take you as my authority that there are bacteria, even though I've never seen one under a microscope. But I can't take you as my authority that Harrison Birtwistle's music is good without actually listening to some. I can understand what bacteria are by getting an entirely abstract account of them. But you can't describe why the *Mona Lisa* is beautiful in the same abstract terms. My aesthetic experience is essentially and wholly *mine*. The idea that I should think something is beautiful because some art critic or style guru tells me to, is, for Kant, complete anathema. He is even more contemptuous of Hume's idea of taste decided by committee than he is of his idea of morals decided by committee. When encountering a beautiful object you don't go about 'gathering votes and asking other people what kind of sensations they are having'[1] But however much my aesthetic experiences are mine they are not, as in the empiricist account, wholly subjective. I don't say that this rose is arousing warm fuzzy sensations in me though I know that in itself it

has all the inspiring qualities of a plastic spoon. I say 'this rose is beautiful'. How are we to explain this strange, subjective objectivity?

Kant makes a distinction between what is agreeable and what is beautiful. I judge an ice cream to be good because I look forward to the pleasure it will give me when I consume it. Aesthetic objects also give me pleasure, but there are two interesting differences. One is that the pleasure is far more intense. The other is that in taking such acute sensual pleasure in a beautiful object I don't consume it. It doesn't conform itself to me as the ice cream does. I conform myself to it. I don't devour it, I contemplate it. The pleasure I get from it is one of appreciating its form, and the harmony and unity of its parts. If I consumed it I'd destroy it. The pleasure you might get from eating a cornetto is sequential. First you sink your teeth into the chocolate covering and get a chocolatey pleasure, then a creamy one, then that plastic-like taste when you get to the cornet. But contemplating beauty is an all-at-once pleasure. You can't actually find the harmony by looking at any one part. If you take it to pieces, as a scientist would, you actually remove it. I don't appreciate it with my body but with my mind, and yet it is an acute sensual pleasure. In aesthetic experiences mind and body, thought and feeling become one. This is one of the things that suggests to Kant that in contemplating beautiful things we are in some kind of direct communion with the super-sensible, the *ding an sich*. We encounter the transcendental realm of intelligence in an actual empirical object with no mediating steps of logical argument or rational investigation. We don't just think about the beauty, as we think about Newton's laws. We eat it, so to speak. We don't say 'I must ask Hume and Burke and, just to make sure, Sir Joshua Reynolds whether this is beautiful or not'. We know immediately that we are in contact with something much more transcendentally ravishing than ice cream. We feel our thoughts.

Because beautiful things are objects in the world just like any other, they come within the scope of Kant's general philosophy. We know them, therefore, through the filter of the mind, but there is, nevertheless, a difference. The imagination is a crucial faculty for Kant because it turns sense data into intelligible experiences, it makes them into pictures and mentalizes them.[2] When I see a dog outside the window I know that it's a dog because I refer the sense datum that my imagination presents to my intellect to the general file marked 'Dog' that I have in my mind. I know physical things by translating them into ideas by the use of my imagination and then classifying them in my mental library of thoughts. I derive a certain satisfaction from my action because all knowledge brings the peculiar pleasure that arises from harmonizing the outer world with my internal filing system. But when I listen to a piece of music it's rather different.

* * *

In listening to the music I also gain pleasure, in fact, if I'm not tone deaf, far more pleasure than I did in knowing that this object is a dog. The pleasure in this case doesn't arise from the kind of satisfaction we get when we find our filing system has worked – thank you Miss Jones, what a treasure you are – but from appreciating the overall form of the piece, its development, its contrasts, the tension between its tone and its rhythm, the unity, in fact, of all its parts. But this unity isn't *there* in any single one of the notes as they sequentially strike my ear. [3] My senses present the notes to my imagination, one damn note after another, just as it presented one damn dog after another. But I don't experience the beauty of the piece as a sequence of notes as I experience the dogs I know as a sequence of dogs. The unity of the piece, that gives me so much pleasure, is a product of my intellect working on the imaginatively processed sense data that have been presented to my mind. It's a consequence of something that has happened inside me. Yet at the same time, I am not at liberty to interpret the notes in any way I want. I can't say, I think I'll hear Bach's Brandenburg No 1 as Beethoven's Emperor Concerto today. Through the notes, my mind apprehends the unity that was already present in the composer's mind. Through the sequential operations of sense a formal reality that transcends sequentiality has passed directly from the composer's mind into my own. There is a meeting, a conformity, of minds.

That wasn't the case with the dog. There the pleasure came from conforming a sensual object to my mind. Here the pleasure comes from conforming my own mind to another. Through art I escape, as it were, from the limitations of my own mind into somebody else's. Through his art the artist, as it were, goes public and makes his own subjective experiences into a kind of object, an actual thing out there, that

transcends both his limitations and mine, and lets both of us out of our subjective prisons. Scientists do this too of course. Newton's laws have moved from the speculative ideas of a private individual into a transcendental realm of objective truth, certain, irrefutable, there for ever. But I can't touch, see and hear Newton's laws. In works of art I can. In science the transcendental is an idea only. In art the escaping from your own mind into an intelligibility that isn't just in your own mind, but out there too, is a tangible reality.

* * *

Kant also has very interesting things to say about beauty in nature as well as in art. He thinks that the beauties of nature are always superior to those of art. This is because in looking at a work of art we always bring a component of intellectual judgment – how well has the artist fulfilled his purpose? But in looking at a rose we never stand back from it in that way. We give ourselves to it entirely. The artist's work is saturated, so to speak, with his intention of making it, whereas a rose is just there. A rose isn't *for* anything. Yet the beauty of the rose is no more in any one of its parts than the beauty of the music was actually *in* the notes.

Its being is wholly physical and yet at the same time its beauty is mental. Just as when listening to the music our minds came into direct contact with the composer's mind through the notes, so in looking at the rose, through its different parts - its stamens and its colour and so on - we come into direct contact with a unity, something mental, an intelligibility that is in the rose. There is intelligibility in nature just as there is in our own minds. But Kant thinks intelligibility isn't something you can parcel up into parts, because you can only do that with material things. So the intelligibility in the rose must be the same as that inside us. There can't be one intelligence inside us and another in the world. In looking at the rose we encounter ourselves. We come into contact with 'the universal forms / Of human nature' as Wordsworth put it. But our minds are essentially purposeful. Everything that we do we do for some reason. We even look at roses *in order* to give us pleasure. But the rose is just there. If the intelligence in nature and that in our minds are the same, yet the intelligibility in our minds is purposeful and that in the beauty of the rose isn't, then what is the answer to this conundrum? Kant gives a really interesting response, as we'll see later. He calls it 'purposiveness without purpose'.

Kant goes on to think about an even more intense form of beauty in nature, what he calls the sublime. As ever, he starts by objecting to both the rationalist position and the empiricist position. The rationalists think the sublime is simply a matter of magnitude, 'grandeur', 'splendour' and 'loftiness'. In other words, a big mountain is more impressive than a small one. Kant rejected this because he thought it didn't take into account our curious experiences of displeasure and fear when we encounter the sublime. On the other hand, the empiricist account is wholly in terms of our own experience. Burke thinks that it arises wholly inside ourselves because we don't understand what we are looking at, it's too much for us. Our experience is one of 'astonishment' mingled with 'a certain degree of horror'. But Kant also rejects this purely psychological account. As Bach's music actually is beautiful so the sublime actually is sublime. Kant thinks that the sublime is always deeply disturbing, we only encounter it when we contemplate 'chaos' in nature, in nature's 'wildest and most ruleless disarray and devastation'. Roses, neatly there in your garden or decorating hedgerows, are never sublime. He thought sublimity came in two forms, in vast magnitude as 'in shapeless mountain masses' or in dynamic form, as in 'the boundless ocean heaved up'.[4]

* * *

Experiences of the sublime occur, according to Kant, when our imaginations, which do a good job on dogs, find the magnitude of the sense datum they are trying to mentalize too much, and fail to present the fullness of what they are trying to grapple with to the mind. When we try and judge such an object 'this judging strains the imagination (as it tries to exhibit the object) to its limit, whether of expansion (mathematically) or of its might over the mind (dynamically).'[5] This is why we feel an element of fear and dismay when we encounter the sublime. Yet, paradoxically, the sublime also arouses in us the most intense pleasure conceivable. Such an experience raises in us 'a feeling of our supersensible vocation'. For the moment, we escape from the person that we are not, as yet, into the transcendental being that we truly are. Within the envelope of your five or six feet of flesh you have inside your head the most wonderful thing in the world, an instrument of infinite capacity that can consider an infinity of numbers, and not only think back to yesterday but think back beyond the immediate past to countless centuries and eons, and beyond that through billions of light years right back to the Big Bang, and even beyond that to puzzle over what can have happened in the time before time began. Yet most of the time our minds are, inevitably, an engine idling, as Wittgenstein said. We aren't thinking about the square root of minus one or what happened before the Big Bang, but whether we can get to the shops in time before they shut and whether we've been overcharged on the electricity bill. But this, surely, is not what this most excellent piece of work – 'how noble in reason, how infinite in faculty, in form and moving how express and admirable, in action how like an angel, in apprehension how like a god' – truly is.[6] In encountering the sublime we escape for the moment into the transcendental 'Being that we truly are'. We don't just think about it. In such experiences we *are* it. In encountering the sublime we know with a unique intensity of feeling that we are transcendental creatures.

What a difference it would have made to *The Origin Of Species* if Darwin had been soaked in Kant. If ever there were anybody capable of writing a Kantian/ Humboldtian *Origin* it was the young Darwin. Here we have one of the very few great writers in history so intelligent and so sensitive he is able to convey to us, directly from his personal experience, that in his analysis of the sublime Kant was right. Darwin's account is exactly that of Kant: the bewildered imagination, the feeling of having been translated onto another plane of being, the enlarged pleasure of confrontation with devastation and chaos, the intense rapture, the extraordinary pleasure that comes from being unable to grasp the fullness of what you are experiencing, the feeling of indisputable transcendence. In Patagonia 'the stillness and desolation' gave Darwin 'inexplicable pleasure'. On top of the Andes he was intoxicated with 'the wild broken forms, the heaps of ruins piled up during the ages'. It was beyond what his imagination could conceive, it was 'a scene I could never have imagined'. What he is experiencing is beyond what his mind can comprehend yet he is, amazingly, comprehending it. In the Cape Verde Islands he notes 'the numberless and confusing associations that rush upon the mind'. In Brazil he confides to his journal 'a glorious day, like giving to a blind man eyes – he is overwhelmed with what he sees and cannot justly comprehend it'. In 'the great, wild, untidy, luxuriant hothouse of the Amazon' his mind was 'a chaos of delight'. 'The delight one experiences in such times bewilders the mind – if the eye attempts to follow the flight of a gaudy butterfly, it is arrested by some strange tree or fruit; if watching an insect one forgets it in the stranger flower it is crawling over'. The cries of the birds and animals are like some great choral evensong that fades, in so Kantian a mode, 'to a universal stillness'. He staggers dizzily 'from raptures to raptures'. Such 'transports of delight' he had never known.

Kant would have given Darwin exactly what he needed. Because of his over-riding metaphor of the plant breeder selecting the best variations, Darwin was committed to a picture of an intelligent agent working on organic material. Yet because of his exclusive familiarity with Paley his concept of an intelligent designer was essentially that of an external contriver outside nature, the very thing that his discovery told him was not the case. It was a hopeless contradiction that, inevitably, could only be resolved by presenting natural selection as an anthropomorphic fiction, an intelligent agent that by definition was not intelligent. And since the plant breeders didn't produce the variations upon which they worked, but only discarded and rejected those that were of no use, Darwin was forced into another contradiction. He was only able to picture natural selection as creating by exterminating. Darwin was determined, in spite of all Wallace's objections, to present man as part of nature and a product of natural selection. Yet in the very act of writing about it he treated nature as an object and distanced himself from it. In *The Descent* he seeks to show man's similarity to the animals by demonstrating how the noblest human behaviours originate in them, but, unwittingly perhaps, then goes on to demonstrate man's difference from the animals by arguing that, unlike them, man progresses through cruelties and genocides. Kant would have released him from all these problems. He would have shown him an intelligence operating not outside but *within* nature that was just what Darwin needed. He would have shown him the identity of man in nature through 'the universal forms/ Of human nature'. He would have enabled Darwin to admit his intense sense of beauty into science. The Herschell/Whewell version of science had no room for the nature that Darwin had actually discovered on *The Beagle*. What he discovered was a nature that was overwhelmingly beautiful, wonderful beyond expression, ecstatic, sublime, arousing raptures upon raptures and transports of delight. But Darwin had no philosophical framework within which he could relate what he had actually discovered to his science. The

English empiricist tradition knew nothing of transports of delight. He wanted to please Herschell and Whewell. So he jettisoned what he had actually discovered in favour of a dismal make-believe facsimile.

2. Humboldt

Why did Darwin couch his thesis that there is no designing God, as Paley had maintained, in language that presents Natural Selection as if it were itself a kind of cosmic deity? Why does his thinking seem to be so at odds with his imagination? For one reason, although he later forsook the influences playing so strongly upon him during the voyage of *The Beagle,* they shaped his imagination so much he was never able to escape their impress.   In sharp contrast to most of the forces that formed Darwin's mind as a young man, there was one other that for a time, during the crucial period of the voyage, pushed all the rest aside. . It was the work of Alexander von Humboldt, the first scientist to attempt a classification of the flora and fauna of South America. Introduced to von Humboldt's extremely long account of his South American voyage, *A Personal Narrative,* by Henslow at Cambridge, Darwin fell in love with it and had already read it twice while an undergraduate.

A personal copy was Henslow's parting gift to him. On *The Beagle,* where he had few books available, it became his bible. He read it over and over, 'again and again reading Humboldt' writes Janet Browne 'until he knew the feelings expressed there as if they were his own'.[7] Humboldt was a very different kind of scientist to those English ones of the Baconian and Lockean tradition. As the title of his book suggests, he saw no conflict between scientific investigation and personal experience. 'I believe from what I have seen Humboldt's glorious descriptions are & ever will for ever be unparalleled: but even he with his dark blue skies & the rare union of poetry with science that he so strongly displays when writing on tropical scenery, with all this falls far short of the truth'[8] wrote Darwin. Humboldt was a product of German *Naturphilosophie.* For him science was as much about the expression of the Kantian sublime in nature as it was about measuring and classifying. Darwin's great fear was that the reality of South America would fail to live up to Humboldt's descriptions.

In fact they far exceeded any merely verbal account, even Humboldt's. During the voyage of *The Beagle,* under Humboldt's influence, Darwin experienced the nature he was discovering more as if it were a religious revelation, an epiphany of the sublime, rather than the impersonal collection of empirical data recommended by Bacon. Under von Humboldt's influence – 'I am at present fit only to read Humboldt; he like another Sun illumines everything I behold...' - what Darwin was paying attention to in the raptures upon raptures and the transports of delight was the beauty of form. At this stage of his career, form was absolutely paramount in his understanding of biology: 'Many of these creatures so low on the scale of nature are most exquisite in their forms and rich colours – It creates a feeling of wonder that so much beauty should be apparently created for so little purpose'. If anybody ever actually experienced the sublime it was Darwin. But 'a world of future and more quiet delight' never arose. What actually did arise was Shakespeare experienced as nauseatingly dull, music that simply confused the mind and substituted misleading feelings for reason, and landscape 'that does not arouse in me the exquisite pleasure that formerly it did'. Why did none of Darwin's South American ecstasy make it onto the pages of *The Origin Of Species*?

The western liberal myth rests on two great founding

scriptures. They are *The Wealth Of Nations* and *The Origin* itself. Both have proved to be exceptionally misleading, but only because both contain great truths that have been grossly distorted and widely misunderstood. In Adam Smith's case his profound insights were not only misread but actually turned into their very opposite by the liberal free trade economists of the nineteenth century, and have largely continued to be so ever since. In Darwin's case his great insight was misinterpreted by himself. But how could it have come about that so great a scientist who wrote so very great a book could have so profoundly mistaken his very own theme? How are we to comprehend this? The impulses that led Darwin not only into making his great discovery but also into perpetrating his great error, become much clearer when we pay more attention to von Humboldt's influence on him – and to English science's profound inability to understand Humboldt and the tradition from which he sprang. But to appreciate Humboldt we have to understand what happened to Kant's ideas when they were re-interpreted by subsequent German philosophers. We need to take into account, too, that there have been very few times when, and places where, there has been an intense intellectual ferment that has inspired and transfigured the people affected by it to a really exceptional degree. One occurred amongst the philosophers and scientists of ancient Athens, another among the dramatists of Elizabethan London, another in fifteenth century Florence, and another in late eighteenth and early nineteenth century Jena and Weimar, from where Humboldt derived his inspiration.

The revolution at Jena was begun by Fichte.[9] Fichte accepted Kant's arguments in general but pointed out that if we have no way of knowing what the *ding an sich* is, how can we know that it exists at all? All we can talk about is what we know and what we know is not the world but our experiences of it. Since all we know is experience, and we can only know the world in the way we experience it. as Kant had pointed out, we have no reason to think that an external world actually exists. It is literally a figment of our imaginations. All that we know is not things but knowledge. It is hardly surprising that we find mathematical laws working in the world as well as in our heads because the world is really inside our heads. We find out truths about the world by deducing them from previous transcendental principles, and it is hardly surprising that we can conduct experiments confirming these principles, because they too are really only exercises in corroboratory abstraction. When Galileo sees his feather and cannon ball dropping at the same speed in a vacuum, and thus confirms his theory by concrete verification, what he is actually seeing is not a cannon ball, as such, at all but the content of his act of sight, his idea of it. We experience transcendental elements present in the world, beauty and mathematics for example, because what we are experiencing is the transcendence of our own minds. Fichte thus opened the way to extreme German idealism, but Fichte in his turn was criticized by his pupil Schelling.

Schelling was far more of an experimental scientist than Fichte. It was clear to him that scientists don't discover the laws of nature by deduction and then confirm them by experiment, it is the other way round. The point of departure and the point of verification, the beginning and end of science, is always that of empirical investigation. Schelling was also more of a poet. Philosophers may be satisfied by intellectual abstractions. Poets deal in concrete feeling truths. Two elements came together in Schelling to lead him on to develop his *Naturphilosophie*. One was his discovery that there are underlying patterns in nature. The other was his response to Kant's immense poetic excitement about the transcendental nature of reason. Kant enthralled people so much because he communicated incomparably compellingly his own sense of the wonder that, in this world of dust and compromises, humanity possesses a godlike and transcendental faculty. For Kant philosophical truths were not simply established, they shone and dazzled and transfigured.

Kant, however, had always been very careful to maintain that we cannot attribute the workings of this godlike faculty that we find in ourselves to the world. We can only act *as if* the world conforms to our experience of space and time, and is ruled by the same mathematical laws that we find in our heads. We can only act *as if* there is a transcendental source for the categorical imperative that we discover in our own moral lives. We can only *believe* that there is a further and all-embracing cosmic teleology underlying and drawing on the limited teleology that we see operating in living organisms such as trees. Schelling took from Fichte the teaching that the world is not only *as if* transcendentally understood, as Kant had maintained, but that its wonder is actually in it, easy enough for Fichte because he thought mind and world were identical. For him, the difference between mind and world is no more than the difference between the mind and its ideas. Schelling now took the step of asserting that there is not only a wondrous and transcendental force of reason working in our heads, there is also a wondrous and transcendental force actually operating in a nature that is out there. And not only that. *They are the same force.*

* * *

In taking this step Schelling was, in fact, being entirely faithful to the spirit of Kant. For Kant's whole point in *The Critique Of Judgment* is that in experiencing beauty we *do* escape from the prisons of our own minds into a direct encounter with beauty itself, the *ding an sich.* Kant, however, had always put the emphasis on the individual experiencing the beauty of this particular rose or the sublimity of this particular mountain. It was Fichte who taught that since there is nothing but mind, and all mind is one, there is really only one transcendental mind expressing itself through the particular cases of all the individuals who have minds. Schelling now transferred this idea of a single sublime force, expressing itself through and uniting together all the particular beautiful and sublime things in the mind, to nature itself. Schelling drew on two areas of evidence to demonstrate his theses. One was the existence of what he was now calling archetypes in organic forms. There is an underlying ideal blueprint beneath every form, however imperfect the actual expression of that ideal might be. The other was the presence of the sublime in nature. Why is nature sublime? Because we see the ideal blueprint shining through the concrete form. In nature you can actually *grasp* the enthralling sublimity of rational truth that Kant had located only in the mind. The equivalent of the uplifting and noble faculty of reason that mankind discovers in itself, we also observe in the noble and uplifting magnificence of the natural world about us. Schelling, however, was not enough either of an experimental scientific investigator nor enough of a poet to take his ideas much further forward. Astonishingly, a man who was both of those things was living in the very next town. He was Johann Wolfgang von Goethe.

When Goethe met Schelling he was already internationally famous for his erotic poems inspired by a string of love affairs. There can have been few men who have ever loved women as much as Goethe – 'the *weiber liebe* that plagues him' as Schiller put it. Already he believed that erotic experiences were incomparably more enthralling than other pleasures because in them, unlike eating or playing chess, a universal beauty that underpinned the whole of nature shone through them. Each woman was incomparably beautiful because in her own unique way she was an expression of what he had already come to call the eternal feminine, the source of the beauty that is to be discovered not just in women, though they are its fullest glory and its crown, but in everything. These ideas of Goethe's were given an immense impetus by his visit to Italy in 1786. Under the warm Italian sunshine they flowered and burgeoned. To start with he was utterly stunned by meeting Emma Hamilton in Naples, the great beauty (from Blackburn incidentally) who was later, of course, to have an equally totally bewitching effect on Nelson. If this wasn't the eternal feminine herself, then ravishing Emma Lady Hamilton was a pretty good evidence for her. Then in Rome he met the love of his life although, unfortunately, we don't know who she was. It came to him like a revelation that experience is one, there is no gap between the intellect and the feelings, poetry does not just talk about experience but is its vessel and realisation. A sentiment that he caught immortally in his lines:

> I have softly beaten out the measure of hexameters
> Fingering along her spine

Perhaps he put it like this because Italy also awakened another interest in him, anatomy. He took to intense and prolonged contemplation in art galleries of the studies of the body that had been made by the Italian old masters of the Renaissance. The beauty of the body, he was coming to see, lay in its underlying organization. The last of the great revelations that Italy bestowed on him occurred in the municipal gardens in Palermo sometime during April 1787. Suppose among this great mass of plants, this museum of vegetable life, there was an example of the oldest plant, the first plant? Suppose all the other plants had developed from that one? Suppose that there was an underlying structure that was common to all plants? While reading in *The Odyssey* the passage where Odysseus is overwhelmed by the beauty of Nausicaa, he conceived the idea of the ideal plant, the *urpflanze,* an archetypal design underlying all plant life.

Goethe could hardly have been better prepared for his meeting with Schelling. Here was the very intellect and the exact philosophy that explained and ordered the insights that he had already developed for himself. A great poet had met a great philosopher and discovered that they were the right and left hand gloves of a pair. It was like two champagne bottles being opened simultaneously. The world that Schelling opened up to Goethe was that of science. He saw, now, that science and art were two complementary faculties, both devoted to revealing the ideal patterning that underlay the sublimity of nature, each of them illuminating the other. Goethe set to work with a will to find evidence that this ideal underlying pattern really did exist. Each part of a plant, he now believed - and thought he could offer experimental evidence to prove it - was an unfolding of a basic structure that was already present in the leaf, repeated in more and more complex and ever new variations in each aspect of the plant as it developed. Originally he had thought that the underlying pattern of the plant was a physical organization, first expressed in the leaf and then in more and more complex forms. A plant was in fact a developed leaf. Now, under Schelling's influence, his thinking began to become more subtle. Now he believed that the *Bauplan,* the underlying pattern, was not physical but metaphysical. It could itself nowhere be touched or seen, but the evidence of its underlying presence was apparent – shining out in its beauty indeed - to the prepared mind and heart in every organ of the plant that it underlay. The title of Goethe's great work on plants *Versuch die Metamorphose der Pflanzen zu Erklaren* really said it all. Plant growth was metamorphosis. It wasn't addition, nor even development, it was unfolding, the ordered manifestation of an unseen animating principle.

* * *

Goethe next turned his attention to animals. There too there was, underlying their forms, an *Archetypus* or *Bauplan.* What the leaf was to plants the backbone was to vertebrates. In every part of a vertebrate animal's anatomy there was an underlying structure that could already be seen in embryo in the backbone, developed and extended in ever more complex and different ways as the animal grew. Goethe's study of animals led him on to fresh insights. Plants, he noted, developed sequentially, one feature of the plant growing out of an earlier one that had preceded it. This can be observed when whole plants are grown from cuttings. The features of a new plant appear one by one from the cutting. What cuttings also show, it seemed indisputably clear to Goethe, is that the essence of the whole plant is already present in the cutting, for otherwise how could a whole new plant grow out of it? It was powerful evidence for the *Bauplan.* There was even more evidence in the animal kingdom. Plants grow sequentially, but the different features of an animal embryo develop simultaneously. This seemed to be an even better argument for an underlying structure that was expressing itself through them. There must be something that was controlling and ordering this simultaneous development. Plants, and animals even more, are organic not only in the sense that each part depends for its sustained being on the activity of the other parts, but in the deeper sense that each part in its own way reveals the same underlying structure that is the very essence of each organism. According to Goethe we can never actually see the *Archetypus,* only the evidence for it, in the metamorphosis of the same underlying structure. Of course, it is more fully evident in the whole animal than it is in its backbone, but it is just as fully present in the backbone as anywhere else. And when we look at the whole animal we are not actually looking at this ideal underlying structure, for it is only visible to the mind, we are only seeing a fuller expression of it.

Goethe's study of anatomy led him to further insights. There is not only a metamorphosis of the underlying *Archetypus* in a single animal, expressed less completely in the backbone and more completely in the whole animal, and evidently present in the anatomical transformations that can be observed, there is also evidence of similar metamorphoses of underlying structure between species. There is anatomical evidence of similar structure in the human hand, the horse's hoof and the sloth's claw.[10] What is seen as a less complete revelation of an underlying ideal pattern in one kind of animal is seen in more complete form in another. As in the individual animal its organic parts are as they are, and deeply interconnected, because there is a reflection of the whole in each part, so in the same way the members of a whole class of animals, such as the mammals, are deeply interconnected by a similar reflection of the deep pattern of the whole genus, the common underlying physical organization, in the different species. There is also a profound connection between the animal and the environment in which it lives. The same ideal pattern is working in the animal as it is in the landscape, and the way of being of the former is shaped by its belonging to the latter. 'There is therefore a truly organic relationship between the mammal and the landscape in which it dwells'.[11] The animal is congruent to, and shaped by, its environment.

There is therefore a hierarchy of expression, lesser and fuller manifestations of an underlying *Bauplan,* in the animal kingdom. It was here that Goethe made contact with another important idea that he got from Schelling that had ultimately been derived from Fichte. Fichte thought that there was a single transcendental mind that was working itself out in ever fuller and more complex manifestations in individual minds through the course of time. (Hegel of course, who during these years was Schelling's next door neighbour, would later take up this idea in a very big way). But given the double focus that was of the essence of *Naturphilosophie,* that there is a corresponding transcendental reality in both mind and nature, it was inevitable that Goethe was going to come to the conclusion that there was a transcendental ideal force working itself out in ever more complex ways, not only in the mind but also in parallel in the development of anatomical forms in nature, over the course of time. These forms were not unconnected. As there was a metamorphosis of leaf into plant and backbone into animal, so that there was an unbroken continuity of expression, each feature intimately and physically connected with its organic counterparts, so there was a continuity between less and more fully developed expressions of the underlying ideal in different species of animal in ongoing time, one developing out of the other and all profoundly connected. Different species do not suddenly appear from nowhere. They develop from the less complete manifestations of the *Bauplan* that preceded them. Goethe had, in fact, thought of evolution, but it was a very different kind of evolution from that which, already before Darwin, had become common intellectual currency in the Anglo-Saxon world. It was not simply an anatomical continuity of which the past manifestations are now stiff, dead and fossilized. It was a gradual revelation of sublimity.

Alexander von Humboldt fell under Goethe's spell. He had been an inspector in the Department of Mines in Prussia, and by the time he arrived with his brother Wilhelm at Weimar in the late seventeen-nineties he was already a considerable experimental scientist in his own right. He had become especially interested in a dispute between the physicists Galvani and Volta. Galvani had shown experimentally that a decapitated frog could be made to move its limbs when a current of electricity was put through it. Galvani believed that there was an endogenous electrical system in the frog that was part of its life force, now revivified by the experiment. Volta, on the other hand, thought that the muscle contractions were being entirely caused by external stimulation. What was at issue was whether there was an internal power, a dynamic Goethean ideal force of which the frog's electrical system was the enabling instrument, or whether, Newtonian-wise, the frog was simply made up of inert particles moved by external forces. Humboldt was thus well prepared for the immense impact that Schilling and Goethe were to have upon him at Weimar. He deeply absorbed the atmosphere of intellectual and emotional excitement that marked the Jena and Weimar philosophers, poets and biologists, and became profoundly imprinted with their ideas. In 1799 he set off on a journey to South America intending to substantiate these ideas with new phenomena hitherto largely unknown to Europeans: that there are underlying patterns connecting different organic forms, that nature is sublime, that the forms of animals are shaped by the environments in which they live, that there is a connection between external nature and the human internal moral life. His journey was to take five years. The title of the book he wrote describing it, *A Personal Narrative,* tells us much about von Humboldt's attitude to science. Together with his other great work *Cosmos,* Humboldt's South American account became the Bible of the Romantic biologists.

In spite of his friendship with Schelling, and the great influence that Schelling's ideas had had upon him, Humboldt was nevertheless quite critical of N*aturphilosophie.* Much later, in 1827 and 1828, he gave a course of lectures in Berlin, exposing the pretentious Fichtean nonsense that accompanied so many of Schelling's ideas, and emphasizing the importance of empirical enquiry and verification in science ('diamond is flint arrived at consciousness', 'America is a female figure, long, slender and icy-cold at the 48th parallel', 'The East is oxygen, the West hydrogen' are among Schelling's more absurd *obiter* *dicta* - English science can almost be forgiven for its rejection of *Naturphilosophie*).[12]   But Humboldt's greatness was to see through and beyond the nonsense, as contemporary English scientists did not, to see that reason and imagination have an equally important part to play in science.   Humboldt came to believe that there were sixteen basic structures to be found in plants.   All species and sub-species were variations on one of these.   He also thought that there was a close connection between botany and geology, that, as Goethe had taught, there is an organic connection between plant and environment.   Similar plants grow in different areas of the world on similar soils.   '..... similar vegetable forms, as pines and oaks, alike crown the mountain declivities of Sweden and the most southern portion of Mexico'[13]   Very important to Humboldt was the idea – and this was pure Goethe of course – that nature should be looked at with an artistic as well as a scientific eye.   Plants should be classified not simply by collating their features, as Linnaeus had done, but also by comparing their aesthetic qualities. The scientist should not only cut the plant up to discover its internal organization, he should also draw it in order to understand how that internal structure expressed itself in the plant's outer form.   Important too was the atmosphere of the place where plants were to be found. The geological, social, economic and atmospheric conditions were all important in communicating not only vegetable types, but the singularity of each type in the place where it was found, and the particular impression that it made on the beholder.   Organic forms were not simply aggregations of inert parts pushed about by Newtonian external forces, and communities of forms - herds, shoals and forests - mere aggregations of similar types, they were all deeply connected to each other by a single great internal essential power that was working itself out in each form and each species in a different way. The whole world was, in fact, a vast system of interconnected phenomena that were all influencing each other, a universal vision Humboldt put forward in his other great work *Cosmos.*

The scientific investigatory journey was also a journey into the moral self, a discovery of the world within that was mirrored by the one without. To become a scientist is to develop the moral life, it is to become a fuller and more extended human being through absorbing the wonders and beauties of nature into one's own person. It is not only to fill the mind, it is to expand the soul. It is to realise that the mind finds itself reflected in nature and nature in the mind, that in fact they are one and the same sublime substance, and it is science that reveals this sublimity. The scientist in his laboratory searches after the transcendentally sublime as does the Carthusian in his cell. The scientific investigator had a duty, not merely to communicate facts to his reader but also the quality of his personal experience, his excitement at the discoveries he had made. His aesthetic impressions were as important as the discovered facts that accompanied them: 'The azure of the sky, the effects of light and shade, the haze floating on the distant horizon, the forms of animals, the succulence of plants, the bright glossy surface of the leaves, the outlines of mountains, all combine to produce the elements on which depends the impression of any one region' [14] With one eye noting and collating both the internal and external features of the organism he was examining, with the other the artist-scientist should contemplate the sublimity with which the ideal pattern, the *Archetypus,* was expressing itself through them. Through investigating nature as closely as possible, the scientist became more acutely aware of its glory, and thus became a more elevated and awakened person, and it was his duty to communicate to the reader not only the factual discoveries he had made, but the uplifting effect that so close a contemplation of nature had had upon him. Nature had an inner heart as well as an outer garb. The naturalist was responding to a vocational call from her, almost as if she were a beckoning goddess, to penetrate to that sublime heart. 'If America occupies no important place in the history of mankind, and of the ancient revolutions that have agitated the human race, it offers an ample field to the labours of the naturalist. On no other part of the Globe is he called upon more powerfully by nature, to raise himself to more general ideas on the cause of the phenomena, and their natural connection.'[15]

Darwin was first introduced to Humboldt's work by his mentor Henslow at Cambridge. Cambridge could hardly have failed to take notice of the great explorer, for he was by now the most famous man in Europe. The scientific spoils of his South American expedition were staggering in their extent. His observation of the Leonids led to the establishment of their periodicity. He discovered that the Amazon and the Orinoco were connected   He reached and located the source of the Amazon. In Colombia he had climbed to what was then the highest point any human being had ever reached, on Mt Chimborozo. He had already established himself as the founder of modern geography. He invented isothermal lines as links whereby the climatic conditions of different countries could be compared. He enquired into the origin of tropical storms, and discovered that the earth's magnetic field declines in intensity as the traveller leaves the poles and draws closer to the equator. We need hardly mention the discovery of the Humboldt current. He decisively solved the long running dispute between those who held that rocks were formed through fire and those neptunians who thought that they were the result of aquatic deposits, in favour of the ignaeans. He showed that volcanoes were to be found in lines following the course of subterranean fissures. It was the naturalist, though, who above all others found a treasure trove of new discoveries in Humboldt's work. He discovered scores and scores of new species, many of which still bear his name: the Humboldtian penguin *spheniscus humboldtii.* a new species of lily *lilium humboldtii,* the South American oak *quercus humboldtii,* to give only a handful of examples. Henslow could hardly have failed, therefore, to be immensely interested in Humboldt's work, but he introduced Darwin to it with a divided voice. On the one hand Humboldt was the very model of an investigative naturalist. On the other, he exemplified that very confusion of subjective emotion with objective research that was anathema above all things to the empiricist tradition in British science. This was not, however, the lesson that Darwin drew. It was the very qualities that Henslow and the Cambridge scientists abhorred that enthralled his pupil. It was Humboldt's aesthetic approach to organic forms, his poetry, the grandeur of the scenery he described, his sense of the great interconnections of nature and his vision of glory that fired Darwin.

Discovering Humboldt's *Personal Narrative* during his first year at Cambridge, Darwin fell in love with it. He copied out long passages to read aloud to Henslow and his friends. Inspired by the great adventurer, he planned a trip to the Canary Islands, to view the volcanoes and the dragon tree that Humboldt had described. But that was not what happened. What did happen was that Darwin was invited to undertake a voyage to the very South America to which Humboldt had journeyed, an excursion that serendipitously was to take five years, exactly the length of time taken by his hero's adventure. Henslow's parting gift to Darwin was a copy of the *Personal Narrative*. It is hardly surprising that Darwin felt Humboldt's guiding hand upon his shoulder. Nor did the voyage disappoint. Its wonders thrown into relief by his sea sickness and the privations of shipboard life, it proved to be even more, far more, than the wondrous Humboldtian experience for which Darwin must have hoped. Shortly after leaving Tenerife Darwin wrote to his father: 'If you really want to have a notion of tropical countries study Humboldt.- Skip the scientific parts and commence after leaving Teneriffe.- My feelings amount to admiration the more I read him.' But Darwin's warm admiration was soon to turn into a kind of ecstasy, almost religious in its intensity. The glowing colours, the luxuriant growths, the soft light filtered through emerald canopies, the awesome cathedral-like silence of the jungles, the sudden cries of strange and brilliantly plumaged birds, the endlessly fascinating animal life, the intoxicating wonder of so wholly new a world whose sensuous touch and seen reality outstripped by far even Humboldt's vivifying pen, the cornucopia of strange and wonderful forms, the intense sensations, the imperative sense of a holy place, the numinous and enthralling revelation of a truly cosmic wonder and glory, all this proved to be a transporting experience far beyond what even Humboldt had prepared him for.

315

'I believe from what I have seen Humbolts glorious descriptions are and ever will be unparalleled; but even he with his dark blue skies & the rare union of poetry with science which he so strongly displays when writing on tropical scenery, all this falls far short of the truth. The delight on experiences in such times bewilders the mind….The mind is a chaos of delight, out of which a world of future & more quiet pleasure will arise.- I am at present fit only to read Humboldt; he like another sun illumines everything I behold'.[16]

It is only when we understand how totally Darwin fell under Humboldt's spell during the *Beagle* years, and how totally that enchantment withered and died once Darwin was back in the dismally grey intellectual climate of England, that we come to see why *The Origin* is so confused a book. Darwin's heart was pulling in one direction, but his head was bidding him go in another. He was, perhaps, a timid man who was peculiarly susceptible to the most immediate influences playing upon him. This was why Humboldt, whose *Personal Narrative* was one of the few books he was able to take with him on his epic voyage - far away from any cold water that the empiricist sceptics in England would scoffingly have poured over it -

influenced Darwin so much in the first place. Back in England he again entered into a scientific atmosphere as unHumboldtian as it was possible to be. The ideas that had been slowly incubating in his feeling life during the voyage, under Humboldt's enlivening influence, did not finally come to conscious birth in his mind until several years after he had returned to England. The midwife who presided over their birth, however, was not Humboldt. It was Malthus. There was one other factor as well that made this painful divide in Darwin into a most grievous wound. He responded with all his heart to Humboldt, but he had virtually no understanding of the philosophical tradition that had produced his hero's inspirations and ideas. His love for Humboldt in his feeling life was intellectually defenceless, even in his own mind. The sad thing was that as the vividly sensed experiences of South America gradually departed from his mind, Humboldt, and the wonder and glory of nature that Humboldt stood for, gradually vanished too. Transplanted back into the intellectual climate from which *The Beagle* voyage had momentarily released Darwin, the Humboldtian vision faded away in the cold and finally died for lack of sustenance. But suppose it had not. Suppose that Darwin had had a philosophical framework within

317

which the glory of nature could have been integrated with natural selection. What difference would it have made?

One stream of influence on Darwin ultimately emanated through Humboldt from Kant, the other from Locke. As it happened Darwin knew almost nothing of Kant but, because it had been a set book at Cambridge, knew long passages of Locke's *Enquiry Into Human Understanding* by heart. Small wonder that the battle between Locke and Kant in his mind was no contest. Darwin shrank before the scathing contempt with which British empiricists dismissed woolly minded, sentimentally vague, cloudy and hopelessly unscientific German idealism. It so happened, too, that Darwin was a totally amateur scientist in a world that was rapidly becoming professionalized. If *The Origin* were to be successful, its author had to please a highly critical professional audience comprised of the greatest British scientists of the day. They wanted facts, proofs, verification, fossil evidence and irrefutable logical deduction. They did not want the cries of South American birds, azure skies, glowing emerald forest canopies and any other wonders that had once turned his mind into a chaos of delight.

The divide between heart and head was made much worse by the unusual fact that Darwin did not actually publish *The Origin* until twenty years after he had conceived its essential idea. During that long period the great vision that had been bestowed upon him, along with his humanity, simply perished. It turned into a merely abstract idea. The most significant thing about *The Origin* was that it was written by a man with a withered heart.

Yet so powerful had been the inspiration of his wonderful adventure, the outlines of the imaginary matrix in which his great idea had first taken shape persisted, even though the intellectual content had now so completely changed. The imaginative form of *The Origin* is completely different, is indeed the opposite of, its scientific thesis. Darwin's book became the classic text of reductionist British biology. It is the supreme example of the application of Baconian method to living forms: the gathering of data, experiment, hypothesis and verification. Yet its essential idea of genius, its wellspring, its key insight, the idea that changes emanating from deep within animals express themselves in organic changes that are then shaped by their environment, comes not from Locke and

Herschell/Whewell but Goethe and Humboldt. This is why it is so confused. This is why Darwin so often writes as if he had been inspired by Kant, in order to put forward ideas whose pedigree ultimately emanates from Locke. It is why this great scientific work is also a great literary work. The ultimate influence of Goethe, reaching Darwin via Humboldt, explains why Darwin proceeds not only by way of evidence, experiment, hypothesis and verification, but also, with the two approaches inextricably entangled, by metaphor. For Goethe art and science are profoundly related approaches. But the fellows of the Royal society did not believe that, nor, by the time he came to write *The Origin,* did Darwin. It is because the German influence and the Anglo-Saxon influence were so confused in his mind that he is never quite sure whether he is speaking metaphorically or factually. His whole point is that there is no designing God in nature, yet he talks about nature itself as if she herself were a designing goddess. It is why nature creates new species, but through an act which is one of extermination. It explains why he presents the development of life as a cold and cruel mechanism, but also portrays it as brought about by a presiding deity who acts like a loving and caring parent. It is why Darwin robs nature of any traces of divine sublimity, yet, especially in his closing paragraphs, presents nature as itself sublime in elevated language worthy of Goethe himself. It is not only that Humboldt's influence never entirely disappears. His presence can still be felt in the very heart of the imagination within which *The Origin* was conceived.

Attempts to present a theory of evolution before Darwin, as in Robert Chambers' *Vestiges,* had done little more than present fossil evidences that showed that the account given in Genesis could not be true. Darwin's theory was vastly superior to these because, unlike them, he not only offered unconnected and incidental evidences, but a driving force that connected and accounted for connections. It was from Humboldt that he derived the idea of an internal driving force, and it was this that led him to his crucial insight that it is the *internal* variations in organisms that really matter, and these that provide the material for natural selection to work on. British science had no understanding of or sympathy for an internal driving force whatsoever. It only understood inert particles moved about by Newtonian external agencies. As a result, Darwin compromised. There was still a creative force, but it was an external one. It was in fact wholly mythical. It was an imaginary invention. There was no evidence for this external driving force whatsoever, nor is there still. This, too, explains why Darwin presented the facts of variation in organisms as if they were *verae causae,* whereas in fact they were no more than observed external regularities. In Goethe's biology it was the *Archetypus* that was the *vera causa,* but the Fellows of the Royal Society were not going to accept that. So Darwin had to find his ultimate explanatory principle for variations somewhere else. Few people, and certainly not the Victorian public, seem to have noticed that mere inductive empirical law, stage two of the Herschell/Whewell scientitific methodology, had been confused with stage three, the deduced *vera causa.*

All this explains too why *The Origin* was such an immense hit with the Victorian public. Given the extraordinary human capacity for self-deception, and the especial need that the Victorians had to deceive themselves into believing that they were not doing what in fact they were doing, the confusions of *The Origin* were exactly the obfuscating inspiration that was required. Mankind is by nature an imaginative species, and therefore cannot operate without myths, but to be effective myths have to be accepted as true. Ever since science began to dethrone the gods, mankind has had a considerable problem in this crucial area. Darwin solved the problem brilliantly. He was able to present what was in fact highly mythical as if it were factual. His patiently assembled factual evidences were enough to convince even the most critical of empiricist reductionists, and this side of his work ultimately derived from Locke. But the sweeping vision, the universality, the imaginative force and the touch of sublimity in *The Origin* came down to Darwin from Kant via Schelling, Goethe and Humboldt. The Victorians not only required compelling evidence that Genesis was not true. Because they were embarked on a great enterprise, setting sail on waters that had previously never been traversed, they also urgently required the sustaining certainty and imaginative inspiration that religions have traditionally given. They required, in fact, a new religion. This was exactly what *The Origin Of Species* gave them. They required a new God, who was no God, who would look upon the world that they had created and find it good. They needed sanction from beyond themselves, to assure them that they were indeed acting well as befitted the pinnacles of creation. They needed a new moral order to approve their deeds. All of these things Darwin gave them by showing that there was no God but only nature, yet by talking of nature as if it were God. Above all they needed a court of mythic permission.

Suppose that Darwin had not been so divided in his mind and had not forsaken Humboldt so completely. What would *The Origin* have been like? There are two areas in particular where it might have been very different. A Kantian vision would have stressed not exterminatory competition but the brotherhood of life, not an external agency but an internal force.

* * *

3. The Brotherhood Of Life

In his chapter on *The Struggle For Existence* Darwin examines the case of an estate in Staffordshire that belonged to a relation of his, where a plantation of Scotch firs had been introduced twenty five years previously into what was otherwise a barren heath.

The change in vegetation within the plantation was remarkable. Twelve species of new plants, not counting grasses, were flourishing in the plantation but could not be found on the heath. There was also a change of fauna. Six insectivorous birds were flourishing in the plantation that could not be found on the heath, even though there were two or three different species of insect eating birds still on the open ground. He discovered an even more dramatic change at Farnham in Surrey. Here extensive parts of a similar open heath had been enclosed, though not for the purpose of growing Scotch firs as in the example from Staffordshire. Here too large numbers of them were springing up spontaneously in the enclosed areas, though only a few in odd clumps on hilltops were to be found outside. On closer examination, Darwin found that there were, in fact, multitudes of seedlings on the open heath, but there they were never able to come to maturity because they were browsed down by cattle. Thus the existence of the Scotch firs here is determined by the existence of the cattle. But in many parts of the world the existence of cattle themselves is determined by other species. In Paraguay there are no wild horses, cattle and dogs, though they swarm in the surrounding countries. This is because in Paraguay there is a certain fly that lays its eggs in the navels of these creatures soon after they are born, which effectively kills them. The flies are held in check by insectivorous birds, but not to the point that it has a great effect on the number of flies. But if there were a great increase in the number of birds, for some reason, it would have a much greater effect, and this would lead to wild cattle appearing in Paraguay, that would in turn graze young trees and thus greatly change the whole vegetation of the country.[17]

The intricate interconnection of species with each other, and their dependence on each other, were recognized by Darwin, and it is for this reason that he is often called the father of ecology. Nevertheless, this is not the main argument that he draws from these examples. Instead, it is the power and ubiquity of the struggle for existence. Of course, it is true that in the examples he describes the different life forms are, to use Darwin's own term, struggling with each other. Some species are denying life to others. But what is equally true is that some are also giving life to others. The presence of Scotch firs in the enclosure of the Staffordshire estate was allowing twelve species of plants to flourish that couldn't be found on the heath.

The navel egg-laying fly in Paraguay was preventing wild dogs, horses and cattle from existing, but it was feeding insectivorous birds. Darwin's observation of facts was marvellous, but the conclusion he drew from them wasn't. Horrified by the cruelty of nature, he nevertheless elevated it into the only natural principle that matters, to the point where it blighted his own inner life and his whole view of the world. But this was a false emphasis and a distortion. Of course, there is plenty of horror and cruelty in nature. But Darwin was led astray by Paley's over-emphasis on nature's smiling face and his explaining away of nature's cruelty, which Darwin rightly saw is feeble, and Locke's false teaching that appearances are misleading while the true principles of nature operate in secret behind them.

* * *

Both doctrines were false. The beauty of nature requires explanation just as much as its horror, although it is difficult to see how these two can be reconciled. In an age of quantum physics it is, perhaps, easier. For us, though few modern biologists seem to have grasped this, the contradictions of quantum has to be science's default position. We cannot see, either, how an entity can be both a wave and a particle at the same time. Yet quantum works. At a profounder level than we can see, nature must be rational. And so it is, perhaps, with nature's beauty and horror. Science itself is driving us out of rational calculation into emotionally coloured guesswork or, as some might like to call it, faith. It is Julian of Norwich's 'all shall be well and all manner of thing shall be well'. Religion's traditional answer has not been that of Paley, it has been the *mysterium tremendum* into which in this life our reasons cannot penetrate. But Darwin had no access to the great central religious tradition of the world. For him religion meant Paley's vacuous optimism, his own family's Christian near-Deism, the unitarianism of the Wedgwoods. No wonder Darwin wanted to give religion up. If his religious background had been richer and deeper he might have interpreted his science very differently. The tragedy of a man who was so exceptionally sensitive to beauty feeling that he had to force himself into discounting it altogether, in favour of the horror he saw so often welling up from beneath his microscope is, surely, one of the greatest in the history of science.

The lesson Darwin might have derived from his

great discovery that all life is deeply interconnected, and stems from a single source, is the brotherhood of all life. He was always confused between two quite different images of evolution, both stemming from his discoveries on the Galapagos. The first is that of evolution proceeding by the invasion of habitats. What he pictured in his mind was seeds and birds drifting on seas and winds from the South American mainland and, because they were better adapted, taking over the islands from their existing inhabitants. Such patterns of evolutionary advance are swift, ruthless and exterminatory. It must have happened thus many times. The whole flora and fauna of the enclosed plantations in Staffordshire had been completely altered within only twenty five years. It is an image associated in Darwin's mind with the dynamism of Victorian England and the rapid expansion of the British Empire. But he also has another picture in mind, of an evolution so incrementally slow that at any one time nothing seems to be happening at all. What he actually found on the Galapagos wasn't evidence of former species that had been exterminated by continental invaders, but finches and turtles that by slow gradation had developed differently in different stations. It is always this vision that was Darwin's true insight, and it is for this reason that Thomson's views on the young age of the earth dealt such a devastating blow to him. For this view of evolution, the slow view, a more appropriate analogy, if we insist on seeing evolutionary change in terms of human societies, would not be the rapidly changing urban societies of the nineteenth century, the competitive image that Darwin projected on to evolution, but the traditional rural ones of the eighteenth.

Picture such a society, gathered round its paternalistic squire, with its hierarchical gradations and its traditional family avocations, one line of descent is wheelwrights for untold generations and another is farriers, each rather better off family customarily rents the same plot of land year after year from the squire, while others, poorer, are totally dependent on the collective rights of scot and lot on the village commons; and thus it has always been since anybody can ever remember. Then think how even a society like this does, nevertheless, gradually change. Every ten years on average a particularly severe bout of tuberculosis coincides with a poor harvest. In such years disease is rampant and food scarce. More old people than usual succumb and their cottages become available to young couples who can now marry and raise families. When the next ten year averagely hard time comes round, the children of a young couple who are now living in a cottage that had been inhabited ten years before by an old person who died in the last cull, are exceptionally vulnerable in the same way the old person had been. Parents struggle desperately to save their children, but some inevitably do not survive. In very bad years, a young married couple may even, with great sorrow, have to decide to concentrate their resources on the child they think is most likely to survive and effectively let the others die. For whatever reason, it is usually the stronger children who do survive, and they who in turn marry and hand on their superior constitution to their descendants. In this way the genetic stock of the village gradually improves, and becomes better able to resist malnourishment and disease by an infinitesimally slow progress. But the lesson we have to draw from this is not that the stronger child who survived, and then handed on his genes, did so because of the pestilence, famine and death that carried off his weaker siblings. He survived because of his parents' care and love. It is not war, pestilence, death and extermination that are the condition of evolution. It's love.

Darwin might have seen this but he did not. It is his

great error. He could have seen it because in *The Descent Of Man* he himself gives us example after example of parental solicitude: Rengger saw an American monkey carefully driving away the flies that plagued her infant, Duvaucel say a Hylobates solicitously washing the face of her young in a stream. Orphaned monkeys are always looked after by foster-parents, Darwin tells us, and the grief of female monkeys who have lost their young is so intense they often die. The driving force that enables the strong to survive, even though the weak succumb, is not competition and extermination but parental solicitude. Even frogs lay their spawn in places where it is more difficult for predators to detect them. Even the ichneumon fly that worried Darwin so much, looked at from another angle as Darwin never did, lays its eggs within the caterpillar with the most tender and solicitous forethought, that its larva may have nourishment readily available when it hatches. Darwin was so blinkered and blinded by social and philosophical prejudices, distorting his vision before ever he looked down a microscope, that he was never able to look at the facts objectively.

Darwin's prejudiced mind is especially in evidence when he discusses Adam Smith. He quotes Adam

Smith's views on sympathy in *The Descent* in support of his thesis that human morality finds its roots in animal social instinct. 'Adam Smith formerly argues, as has Mr Bain recently, that the basis of sympathy lies in our strong retentiveness of former states of pain or pleasure'. Hence 'the sight of another person enduring hunger, cold, fatigue, revives in us some recollection of these states, which are painful even in idea. We are thus impelled to relieve the sufferings of another, in order that our own painful feelings may be at the same time relieved.' Darwin then goes on to say 'But I cannot see how this view explains the fact that sympathy is excited, in an immeasurably stronger degree, by a beloved than by an indifferent person. The mere sight of suffering, independently of love, would suffice to call up in us vivid recollections and associations. The explanation may lie in the fact that, with all animals, sympathy is directed solely towards members of the same community, and therefore towards known and more or less beloved members, but not to all the individuals of the same species. This fact is not more surprising than that the fears of many animals should be directed against special enemies. Species which are not social, such as lions and tigers, no doubt feel sympathy for their own young, but not for that of any other animals. With mankind... those communities which included the greatest number of the most sympathetic members, would flourish and rear the greatest number of offspring'.[18]

Darwin shows in this passage how totally and completely he had misunderstood Adam Smith. Darwin reversed Adam Smith completely. By sympathy Adam Smith always means a love that is potentially universal. Through the development of 'the man within the breast' that occurs as a consequence of my intercourse with my fellow intelligent beings, I rise from a condition of natural biological selfishness to a transcendental humanity. I not only care about the injury to my thumb, or even to the thumbs of my immediate family, I begin to care about the starving in China. Darwin never shows any understanding of so universal a sympathy. He always means a genetic selfishness that is never extended beyond our own immediate group. He might have seen his error here too, for in *The Descent* he gives us example after example of sympathy felt not by human beings but by animals, and offered not only beyond their immediate kin to other members of their species, which on another page he says they never do, but even to beings belonging to other species altogether. Not only does a prime male baboon, 'a true hero', go back to rescue another baboon who is stranded on a rock assailed by wild dogs, a little American monkey, at great risk to his own life, distracts a fierce baboon away from a keeper, thus saving the keeper's life. The little American monkey *was a warm friend of this keeper.* Darwin himself had seen a dog who never passed a cat who lay sick in a basket, and was a great friend of his, without giving her a few licks with his tongue. He saw somebody pretending to beat a lady who had a timid little dog on her lap. '...the little creature instantly jumped away, but after the pretended beating was over, it was really pathetic to see how perseveringly he tried to lick his mistress's face and comfort her'. There was the case too, 'which everybody will remember'. of the dog who licked the hand of the vivisectionist.

It is striking that all these stories where animal sympathy crosses species boundaries occur in cases where individual animals had been, for a long time, closely associated with man. Darwin would doubtless have explained them, as would most biologists today, by saying that long familiarity had effected a transfer of genetic identification. The dog's owner has become a substitute for the pack leader. But how do they know that this is all there is to it? Where Darwin is so superior to most modern biologists is in his skill as a writer. We are, after all, dealing here with one of the great masters of English letters. What he makes us feel so much is the nobility of these animals. What so great a writer might have done, but did not, was to show how not just reciprocal altruism but a noble Smithian universal sympathy is rooted in animal behaviour. If animals are naturally noble, then how much more so should man be? How noble is a man who is concerned about the pinpricks of himself, his children and neighbours, but totally unconcerned about starving people in China? On what a different track Darwin might have set evolutionary biology.

Throughout *The Descent* Darwin avoids the challenge of dealing with universal sympathy, and it is hard not to think this evasion is at least quasi-deliberate. As an example of the compassion felt and practised by civilized men, so at odds with the values of natural selection, he notes that 'we civilized men' shelter the indigent poor in workhouses. But Darwin knew very well that in workhouses husbands were separated from wives and children from parents. Wasn't this the very behaviour Darwin had condemned so vehemently in Patrick Lennon? 'Picture to yourself' he had written in anguish, 'the chance, ever hanging over you, of your wife and your little children – those objects which nature urges even the slave to call his own – torn from you...' Where had all the fire and passion of the young man gone? Darwin's answer to the old Malthusian problem of the poor breeding so prolifically is, effectively, that fortunately the poor die in far greater numbers, and this evens things up. How could he, of all people, have been so cold-blooded? He must have known that the poor feel anguish over the loss of their children just as much as he had done over the loss of Annie. In their case their anguish was worse, for they lost children far more frequently, and were not even able to hope for their recovery by taking them to Dr Gully in Malvern. Darwin sealed himself off from the sufferings of the Irish in Victorian England, the Little Ireland in Manchester described so vividly by Engels, by surrounding himself with fortified thickets of prejudice and stereotype. "The careless, squalid, unaspiring Irishman multiplies like rabbits" Mr Greg is noted with approval as saying (if one can be forgiven for quoting this passage yet again, so neatly does it encompass the smugness that invests *The Descent Of Man*) compared with "the frugal, fore-seeing, self-respecting ambitious Scot, stern in his morality, spiritual in his faith, sagacious and disciplined in his intelligence..."

* * *

The potato famine came particularly close to Darwin. Not only in Ireland but in England too the dependence of the poor on bread and potatoes brought famine right up to the doors of Darwin's own home. Even in Kent work was scarce and the poor were starving. Workmen working on renovating Downe House bickered so much that his foreman, John Lewis, fired the lot. One workman broke down completely, as Darwin vividly described it to Emma: 'his wife had come from a distance with a Baby & is taken very ill – The poor man is crying with misery'. [19] The soft-hearted Charles persuaded Lewis to take him back again. He agreed with Henslow 'about gentlefolk not buying potatoes'. Emma took to giving away penny bread tickets at the door that could be exchanged at the village bakery. All this local suffering touched Darwin deeply. But the sufferings of the three-quarters of a million who starved to death in Ireland, and the million who were forced to emigrate, largely passed him by. Much preoccupied with the sex life of barnacles, he was content with the Whig party line that it was all the fault of the Corn Laws. Was he outraged by Lord John Russell withdrawing even the government-bought maize that Peel would have distributed free in Ireland? The biographers do not mention it. He was willing to abrogate the principles of free trade in the case of the man John Lewis had fired, but not in the case of Ireland. It is an application of his comment on Adam Smith: 'But I cannot see how this view explains the fact that sympathy is excited, in an immeasurably stronger degree, by a beloved than an indifferent person'. But, many years before, his sympathy had been excited to an immeasurable degree by the screams of a tortured slave who, far from being beloved, he had not even seen but only heard. And what are we to make of a man who is greatly disturbed by the sufferings of the caterpillar in whom the ichneumon fly lays its eggs, but not by the sufferings of the Irish? Ireland was, after all, a lot closer than China. Perhaps it would not have mattered if Darwin had had no more nor no less sympathy for suffering humanity than the average Victorian, if he had been an average Victorian. But he was not.   He was a man of exceptional humanity, whose humanity was lost first to himself and then to the world.

Darwin's account of the decline of native populations is equally callous. All he gives us is cold statistics, and no hint of feeling for the terrible tragedies that they conceal. What he was saying, in effect, was that there was no need for the European colonizers to exterminate the natives, although or perhaps because their extermination is exactly what might be expected from the workings of natural selection, nor to feel guilt about these astonishing racial deaths, for natural selection, which is after all the law of nature, will perform the task for them. But natives lying down and dying before the onset of Europeans was not a law of nature. The South American natives did not die like flies on the Jesuit *reducciones* in Paraguay. Nor was there a steep population decline in India, which was only ever half-colonized anyway and where, the colonizers being so few and the natives so many, it was impossible to do much else than allow the peasants to carry on under the British much as they had done under the Moghuls. The peoples who declined so precipitately in the British

Empire did so because, as Darwin's theory predicted, they could not adapt to the new situation that had been imposed upon them. In terms of feelings and emotions they died of despair. Perhaps even without genocides the decline of hunter-gatherer populations was inevitable. The natives' need for large unfenced areas over which to roam and the colonists' desire to fence and farm the same land were irreconcilable.

* * *

Darwin refers to 'the famous hunt' in Tasmania as if he is talking about a celebrated meet of the Pytchley or Quorn. In fact, some Australian historians argue today that the genocides in Queensland and Tasmania have been greatly exaggerated. Perhaps they have, but this hardly turns the story of the Australian aboriginals into a happy one. It is the complete vulnerability of the natives, their inability to understand what was happening to them and the completeness of their precipitate decline that - like Darwin's tales of the pinioned goose who tried to start out on his thousand mile migration on foot and the little dog who didn't understand that his mistress was acting a part but licked her face nevertheless - that makes their history so poignant. Darwin must have felt that poignancy especially intensely, for he visited Tasmania only two years after the last pathetic remnant of aboriginals had been taken to Flinders Island. He was deeply disturbed by the absence of natives. It must have been as palpable as John Lewis's hired man's tears in his own drawing room. But this dreadful knowledge did not prevent him from accepting hospitality from the Surveyor-General George Frankland, with whose family he spent 'the most agreeable evening since leaving home'.[20] Tasmania, he thought, might be a most pleasant place to retire. He solved his emotional problem, as he might have said, by 'adapting'. The truth was that Darwin, he of all people, this most sensitive and kindly of men, shut his heart to his own humanity.

* * *

Darwin was like an inveterate smoker who is so addicted that he cannot give up gradually by half-measures. He was so exceptionally sympathetic it was all or nothing. He chose nothing, and the price paid both by himself and the world was great. What a book he might have written and how close he came to doing so. He was one of the great writers of the nineteenth century. He was a man of an exceptionally feeling intelligence. He had made one of the greatest scientific discoveries of all time. He showed, indisputably, that mankind is one species. He showed too that humans are all descended from the same origin, and are therefore not only connected to the whole of the rest of the web of life but close brothers in the flesh. Whereas Adam Smith had seen sympathy as the prerogative of human intelligence, Darwin showed, brilliantly, that it is rooted in nature. He showed that animals are not mere base brutes but heroic, solicitous and tender. How much more heroic, solicitous and tender might human beings be, then, in their natural state. It was not that he should have published inflammatory pamphlets, necessarily, about British imperialism in Tasmania. Or even that he should have striven to raise awareness about the sufferings of the aboriginals and the Irish. What he might have done was to have established sympathy and fellow-feeling as the default condition of mankind. Both his theory and his personal experience could have told him that 'the same community' within which animals direct sympathy is, in the human case, the whole of humanity. Instead he chose to write a book commending war, famine, disease and death. The 'real world', as he came to see it, is not one of sympathy and feeling - such emotions are to be reserved for light novels, if about a pretty woman 'so much the better' – but one of competition and extermination. When it came to it he was stifled and overcome by the prejudices of his time.

* * *

4. Inwardness.

If Darwin had been more familiar with Kant he would have benefited most especially, for in the last part of *The Critique Of Judgment* Kant deals directly with the very subject that is at the centre of the knot of problems Darwin was wrestling with, that of teleology. By teleology the English scientific tradition meant evidences of a designer in nature, whose purpose was to demonstrate the perfection and goodness of the divine creator who had contrived it. That was not what Kant meant. What Kant meant was not an externally instilled purposefulness that could be theoretically deduced from the observation of nature, but an internal purposefulness that could be inductively perceived within nature. He begins by noting that Newtonian science is of its essence mechanistic. It pictures the world as made of inert particles of matter moved by energetic forces that obey absolute laws. Scientific progress lies in discerning what those laws are. This works extremely well for inanimate objects, but Kant thinks that animate objects are quite different.

He compares a tree with a watch – and what influence this might have had on Darwin, who was already so familiar with Paley's watch, had he read it. In a watch one part makes other parts move, but it is not the cause of the other parts, even though one part is there for the sake of another. Nor is one part there as a result of the other. It is only there because some outside agent put it there. Still less does one watch produce other watches, and if a part breaks down it has no power to replace that part itself. A mechanical device like a watch, in fact, is unthinkable except as the product of an outside agent. Kant thinks that the remarkable thing about organisms is that they actually and exactly *do* do all these things *for themselves*, things that a watch can only do if it has been primed by its designer. A watch is an effect of an external cause. But a tree is its own cause and its own effect. A watch cannot generate another watch. But a tree generates another tree according to its own species. From the point of view of trees as a species, the species is both cause and effect of itself. The acorn is the cause of the oak and the oak is the cause of the acorn. Secondly, the tree also reproduces itself as an individual. It gives birth to another tree that is like itself. Unlike a mechanism, it takes nourishing elements from the air and the soil and *turns them into itself.* It grows. A mechanism can only grow by becoming physically bigger, if some outside agent adds more matter to it. But in living things '…the separation and recombination of this raw material show that these natural beings have a separating and forming power of very great originality: all our art finds itself infinitely outdistanced if it tries to reconstruct these products of the vegetable kingdom from the elements we obtain by dissecting them, or for that matter from the material that nature supplies for their nourishment'.[21] Moreover, there is a mutual interdependence between the different parts of the tree. The trunk needs the leaves and the leaves need the trunk. In the watch the springs need the coil and the coil needs the springs too, but it cannot grow these things for itself. The tree can. This is another sense in which the tree both produces and sustains itself. Added to this, living things have a marvellous ability, as watches have not, to grow new parts for themselves if one of their limbs or organs has been cut off.

These qualities of living organisms are so wonderful, Kant thinks, and so different from those of inanimate matter it is absurd to think that they can be explained by the mechanistic ideas of external forces acting on inert matter, as the behaviours of merely physical objects can be. Living things act purposefully. There is plainly a teleology in nature, which is not that of the theoretical and theological kind so familiar in nineteenth century English science, but palpably and scientifically observable. Yet organisms are also physical objects taking up space in the world. In so far as this is true, mechanistic laws apply to them just as much as they do to any other physical object. Living things, therefore, have to be judged by two sets of laws, mechanistic ones and teleological ones, but they can never be fully explained by a purely mechanistic science. Even a blade of grass cannot be explained only in terms of external forces acting on inert matter, and therefore there can never be, says Kant, a Newton of the grass blade. Kant then goes on to pose the question: if living organisms are teleological, should we say that the whole world is? He certainly thinks that it is reasonable to think so, but the teleology of living organisms, although purposeful, only has the purpose of the preservation of themselves, not the purpose of demonstrating the existence of an outside designer. In this sense Kant's teleology is the polar opposite of Paley's. We can actually observe teleology in organisms, but we can not observe teleology in the world as a whole, any more than we can observe causality when one of Hume's cues is in immediate and prejudicial proximity to a billiard ball. A completely teleological world can therefore never be more than a reasonable hypothesis. Organisms are of their nature purposeful, but they have no other purpose than to sustain themselves. It is this that Kant means by purposefulness without a purpose.

Darwin never even mentions Kant's ideas in *The Origin Of Species,* presumably because he didn't know about them, let alone refutes them. Becoming the Newton of the grass blade was, of course, precisely what he *was* trying to do, but this involved him in a hopeless contradiction. Intellectually, Newtonian mechanism drove him to treat living organisms exactly as if they were inert material particles pushed round by law-bound physical forces. The only such force he could find was natural selection which works on organisms exactly as if they are entirely passive objects, scrutinizing, selecting and discarding. On the other hand, far from regarding them as inert packages of matter, he treats living organisms as if they are not just plants and animals but intelligent agents. They fight wars, compete, adopt strategies and out-manoeuvre each other. He was never able to make these two sides to his theory match up. Imagine what Newtonian physics would look like if each of the atoms that compose matter was following its own agenda and they were all fighting each other. Darwin never resolved another muddle either. He never regarded evolution as the wholly soulless, purely algorithmic affair that, say, Daniel Dennett does. Darwin always wanted a replacement for the traditional religious way of looking at nature that was *as if* religious and yet not religious. He consistently talks about natural selection as if it is a god. Hence his ambiguity about religion and his long, hesitant agnosticism. He was unable to think of nature except in some way that was teleological. Hence the action of natural selection in guiding nature to achieve its own purposes, i.e. the production of the most perfect organisms; otherwise for what else does natural selection scrutinize the field of living things with so eagle an eye? Yet at the same time Darwin wants to say that evolution is blind, there is no sense in which it has a final purpose in mind. It is only a happy accident that it has produced such pinnacles of perfection as the middle class Victorians. Kant's 'purposiveness without a purpose' would have spoken to just these ambiguities that Darwin felt so keenly, and would have released him from the contradictions that he never resolved.

The Newtonian approach that Darwin had learnt from Herschell and Whewell, with its emphasis on external forces, prevented him from appreciating the implication that underlies the Kantian approach, the insight that the forces that move living things come from within themselves. Living things have a 'within' and inanimate things do not. This is the greatest distinction between them, but Darwin missed it completely. This is exactly what his theory of variations might have suggested to him, had he not been so misled by the prejudices of his upbringing. The genius of his insight, that nobody had seen before, was that development in living organisms comes about through a combination of changes within themselves interacting with changes in the environment in which they exist. This is exactly what happens in the case of the plant breeders, and Darwin saw that it is also what happens in nature. Hence the central importance of the metaphor of the plant breeder in his whole scheme. But having seen that both are of vital importance in explaining evolutionary change, both the variations and the environment, he devotes only two sentences to the inner changes, at the beginning of his chapter on *The Laws Of Variation,* where he tells us that we are wholly ignorant of what they are, and then spends the rest of the chapter undoing the truth of his insight by telling us just what they are at great length, obscuring the fact that he has actually substituted externally observed regularities for analysed internal laws. Darwin completely distorts the balance of internal change and external impact, putting so much emphasis on the latter that he is driven to attribute to it powers of agency that it could not possibly have, and virtually completely ignoring the former, even though, as we now know from modern genetics, it is by far the more important of the two partners in the relationship.

At the beginning of the chapter on *The Laws Of Varation,* Darwin says 'I have hitherto sometimes spoken as if the variations – so common and multiform in organic beings under domestication, and to a lesser degree to those in a state of nature – had been due to chance. This, of course, is a wholly incorrect expression, but it serves to acknowledge plainly our ignorance of the cause of each particular variation'. Having admitted that he and the scientists of his time are driven by ignorance to talk of variations as if they come about by chance, he then ignores this proviso and goes on to talk about them as if they were wholly explicable by rational laws that are thoroughly ascertainable. They are such laws as the effects of constant use of a limb or organ that tends to develop it and regular disuse that tends to atrophy it; long inhabiting of a particular environment leading to acclimatization to it, so that plants growing in a cold climate, for example, lose the capacity to survive in a warm one; correlation, whereby a change in one feature of an organism often leads to a corresponding change in another, although the second feature may have nothing directly to do with the circumstances that have changed the first; a part that develops to an extraordinary degree in a species tends to be highly variable, thus leading to more varied offshoots than is usual; a variation in a species often develops characteristics already observable in an allied species, or suddenly reverts to characteristics that had appeared to be long lost; and so on.

* * *

All this is extremely misleading. It treats the variations entirely as if they happen on the outside of the organism, and acknowledges no sense that they result from hidden changes occurring deep within: as if it is nothing to do with what goes on inside muscles, but simply by never taking any exercise you find your muscles have become weak; or if you go on a holiday to India England seems unusually cold when you return, or if you do exercises to improve your control over your feet when dancing you also find that your back has co-incidentally been strengthened, or if you develop your skill as an actor you find it very useful in other walks of life too, or if after many years of not riding a bicycle you find that after all this time you haven't lost the trick of it. All of these are perfectly valid observations, but they don't *explain* anything. The way in which Darwin presents his laws of variation makes them susceptible of just such externalist explanations. He presents them as if they are the true explanatory laws of variation, the *verae causae*, whereas in fact that is precisely what they are

353

not. They are merely examples of the empirical kind of law, the observation of regularities in apparently random phenomena that Herschell defined as merely preliminary to the true deduced *verae causae* that explain why the regularities occur as they do. In this absolutely crucial area Darwin did not explain the causes of variation at all, but misleadingly gave the impression that he had done.

This, again, was a tragic irony, for it was his realization that it was variations occurring within organisms, and the relation of that crucial insight to the environment, that distinguished his theory from all previous hypotheses about evolution. This quality of having a 'within' is a defining mark of life. In the simplest form of a living cell we find rudimentary self-replicating equipment enclosed within an encircling membrane. In eukaryotic cells we find a nucleus within the already enclosed cell, with its own membrane. Within the cell too there are other internalised membrane-surrounded organelles like the mitochondria. Even the simplest kind of organic forms are guided by instincts within themselves to seek food and light. More complex organisms develop a still more intensive form of inwardness, and become more fully self-directing through nervous systems and brains. Higher animals become more and more fully conscious. Finally human beings evolve who are reflexively self-conscious. There has thus been a continuous internal evolution of awareness, feeling and consciousness within organic physical development. Darwin largely misses this. In *The Descent* he shows us animals behaving in ways that if they were human we would say were of the highest ethical calibre. He attributes these behaviours entirely to social relationships, as if they had nothing to do with what was going on inside the animals at all, but only to the way they relate externally to each other. This emphasis becomes most damaging when he comes to man.

In *The Descent* he acknowledges than human beings should be kind to each other. We should reverse the action of natural selection by building workhouses for the indigent and sanatoriums for the sick, and in fact we can congratulate ourselves (smugly and pompously one might feel) that we do. In Darwin's picture, however, it is not moral sympathy that is the real engine of human progress, but external laws, though in fact these are quite bogus. Civilization comes to primitive lands because a natural law decrees that savages become infertile when superior races appear. The middle classes are able to continue to bear their burden of carrying the torch of natural selection because low life Irish children die in large numbers and therefore fail after all to swamp their betters. He has no sense that there are inner laws as well as outer ones. His lack of emphasis on the evolutionary continuity of the inwardness of life led Darwin to discount our moral relationship with the rest of sub-human organic life, and our moral responsibility for it because of our moral kinship with it, despite the fact that he gave so much evidence for it, and so wonderfully, in *The Descent.* As a result, we don't see nature as a brotherhood. We see it as a resource to be exploited. Above all we do not see ourselves as all members of a particularly close evolutionary family, we see other human beings, or at least those not in our immediate circle, as resources to be exploited too. We do not see ourselves as, above all else, universally sympathetic moral agents, as Adam Smith did. We see ourselves as economic particulates pushed about by laws of supply and demand. The true implication of Darwin's discovery was that human behaviour cannot be explained entirely in terms of external forces. The increasingly intensive inwardness of organic life is what, above all, needs to be explained. What Darwin might have seen, too, is that this inwardness has become so intense in man, one could perhaps even say that the evolutionary implication is that human beings have souls, if by soul you mean a particularly intense form of internal self-motivation. Instead we increasingly see ourselves as complex computers. Darwin emphasized external law at the expense of inner richness and moral responsibility. It is an attitude that allowed the Victorians to see their extraordinary feat of appropriating a third of the countries of the globe as an expression of natural law.

(Endnotes)

1   Immanuel Kant. *Critique Of Judgment* section 281. Hackett Publishing 1987. Indianoplis/Cambridge

2   This is the reverse of what happens in the cell, where the non-physical, the information in the DNA is turned into the physical. The messenger RNA takes the purely informational code of the DNA out through the wall of the cell's nucleus into the cytoplasm, where it binds onto a ribosome that in turn binds onto an amino acid, thus turning a pure abstraction into a physical thing.

3   I am indebted to Roger Scruton 1982 *Kant.* OUP for many of these ideas.

4   I am indebted here to Werner S. Pluhar's Introduction
    to the 1987 edition of Kant's *Critique Of Judgment*
    trans' Pluhar and published by |Hackett
    Publishing, Indianapolis
5   *Critique of Judgment* sect. 27 *On the Quality of the Liking
    in our Judgment of the Sublime*
6   Shakespeare *Hamlet*
7   Browne *op cit* p.216
8   quoted in Browne p. 211
9   Most of my information and ideas in this chapter have
    been taken from Robert J. Richards. 2002. *The
    Romantic Conception Of Life: Science and phliopsophy
    in the age of Goethe.* Chicago. Univ of Chicago Press.
10 Henri Bortoft 1996. *The Wholeness Of Nature:
    Goethe's Way of Science* . Floris Books New York
    pp. 275-289
11 Bortoft *op.cit.* p. 97
12 Douglan Botting 1973. *Humboldt And The Cosmos*
    Sphere Books London. P.232
13 Von Humboldt *Views Of Nature.* tr. E.C.Bott and
    Henry Bohn (London Henry Bohn 1850). P. 218
14 *op.cit.* pp 217-218
15 Humboldt *A Personal Narrative* tr. Helen Williams
    7 vols (London Longman 1818-29). 1:xlv-xlvi
16 C. Darwin *Beagle Diary* ed. R. Keynes
    Cambridge, CUP 1988. p.42
17 *Origin* p.123
18 *Descent* p.109
19 Desmond and Moore p.334
20 *ibid.* p 179
21 *Critique* sect. 65 *Things Considered as Natural
    Purposes are Organized Beings*

Postscript

The Darwinian Tragedy

If the *Origin Of Species* was not a disaster for mankind, it was certainly no unmixed blessing. The terrible irony is that it was written by the dearest and gentlest of men, who, if he had written it twenty years earlier, had been better equipped philosophically, and had not been so infected, one might almost say poisoned, by the Malthusian ideas he imbibed at Erasmus's table, might well have written the great Humboldtian work that *The Origin* could have been. He so very nearly saw that the true implication of his own great discovery is that human beings are biological relatives united by love, rather than evolutionary, even at the margin exterminatory, competitors divided by strife. But he did not. Worse, he failed to appreciate that, in showing that human beings are not a special creation but complex animals, his works would become a court of mythic permission for brutal behaviours far more horrific than that found in any brutes. The genocides of the Kasakela chimpanzees have been outdistanced by many millions in the human ones of the twentieth century. In mankind we have an extra-ordinary evolutionary contradiction. An animal body that is descended from animals, as Darwin saw, houses a mind of infinite capacity, as Kant saw. Whereas squirrels only want the nuts that they need to carry them through the winter, and owls only want the mouse that will provide today's meal, human beings want everything, or as much of everything as they can get. Every economics textbook starts with the truism that whereas resources are limited human desires are infinite. Darwin fatally uncoupled mankind from the transcendence that had always been at the heart of western philosophy and culture before it reached its most explicit expression in Kant, and left man with nothing but an infinite desire to compete for limited material resources. It is a philosophical predicament made for trouble. Darwin slew transcendence. He turned his back on Adam Smith's universal sympathy and Kant's transcendental imperative to tell the truth and love one's fellow rational creatures, in favour of a morality that was a local, relative, racial and accidental product of natural selection: Hindus feel guilty if they eat forbidden foods, Thugs feel guilty if they fail to strangle strangers, Victorian gentlemen feel guilty if they fail to write thank you letters after dinner parties. Morality is a social accident that just happens to be what you do. But once *The Descent Of Man* has revealed this to you, why then…

Almost as a facetious joke, Darwin speculates that if mankind had descended from bees, mothers would feel an obligation to kill their daughters and women would feel an obligation to kill men once their breeding usefulness was over. The concept of natural selection enabled him to contemplate, or at least glimpse, a moral schema completely different from the civilized benevolence that ruled at Downe House. At Auschwitz this different moral schema, so imaginary to Darwin it was almost laughable, was exactly what came to pass. The SS doctors who did the selecting for the gas chambers were not moral monsters. They did not think of themselves as committing a crime, but as fulfilling a moral duty. They were human beings who stifled their natural feelings of pity, often at great personal cost, in order to fulfil what they had been taught was a higher moral obligation dictated by natural selection.[1] They were completely wrong of course, and the utterly horrified Darwin would have been the first to say that they were. He cannot be blamed for Nazism. There were many other components in its philosophy apart from Darwinism. But he cannot be exonerated from all responsibility either. Evil men need only the flimsiest of permissions to commit evil deeds, let alone one that appears, falsely but so easily, to emanate from a great scientific truth.

If you teach that nature both exterminates weak races and preserves strong ones, and that man is entirely a product of nature, then it is hardly surprising if the ultra-logically minded draw the conclusion that the extermination of the weak by the strong is mankind's natural moral condition. In *The Descent Of Man* Darwin dodged the issue. On the one hand 'we civilized men' save many of the poor from death through our charity. On the other, sympathy is restricted to one's immediate circle. But if the world is ruled by natural selection, the implication is that those outside the immediate circle of sympathy are subject to it. Darwin wants to eat his cake and have it. He obscures the issue by pointing to the hospitals and the innoculations with which, in Britain, the charity of the rich ameliorated the sufferings of the poor. But a strict Malthusianism would have condemned this, and Darwin never condemns Malthus. There is nothing in the way Darwin interpreted his discovery that would imply that such kindly behaviours are native to human beings. Because in so many parts of the British Empire the fertility of the native populations declined so drastically, thus solving the colonizers' problem for them, Darwin was able to avoid the most inhumane implications of the application of natural selection to the human case, but others did draw it. Were imperialists ever justified in removing the natives they had conquered from the earth, or at least depriving them of their land? In view of the mythic status that he had achieved, Darwin has to take some responsibility for his lack of clarity. Suppose that the Victorians had taken the provision of health to the Irish poor in Manchester so seriously that the child death rate dropped dramatically, thus neutralizing his argument that the superiority of the middle classes was maintained because of the much greater death rate amongst the poor. What would he have said?

* * *

In *The Descent* he did not uncouple human

behaviour from natural selection nearly as clearly as he might have done, and it was this lack of clarity that has allowed the genociders to misinterpret him. Why did he, so kindly a man, not wrestle with this dismally gruesome implication in the way that, most admirably, Richard Dawkins does? Huxley, after all, campaigned as vigorously against Social Darwinism as he had striven to support Darwin. But it was Darwin's name that was the carrier of myth, not Huxley's. Above all, Darwin was handicapped by his prejudice. When it came down to it he was a provincial Victorian through and through. If he had argued against Kant's teleology as effectively as he argued against Paley's, that would have been fair enough. But he did not even mention it. English science was so grandiose, pompous and complacent it did not even deign to notice what had been going on elsewhere. "The careless, squalid, unaspiring Irishman multiplies like rabbits…" The unthinking condescension in this kind of thinking underpinned the racism that disfigured the later British Empire, and pointed the way to the tragedy that lay ahead.

The Origin was an immense loss to literature. What a book this great writer might have written if he had been inspired by a Kantian enthusiasm for the sublime, as Humboldt was, and as he himself had been inspired by Humboldt, twenty years before. How might a Kantian approach have enabled him to integrate beauty with science, and how much a Baconian/Lockean one stifled any possibility of that. *The Origin* was a loss, too, to religion. Because of the smug parochialism of his background, Darwin never realised that Paley's version of religion was not that of any of the great religious traditions, indeed it was almost the opposite. To the Victorians Paley's was the very voice of religious orthodoxy. In fact it was nothing of the kind. None of the great traditions of the world have believed in God because they were so impressed with the ingenuity of the contrivances of nature that they argued to a great external contriver outside it. They have worshipped the divine because they sense a numinous presence, not without the world but within it, both in the natural things about them and in their own hearts. The paleolithic peoples performed religious rituals in caves deep inside the earth. The Neolithic age reshaped the landscape into great natural temples. For the Greeks every river, stream and mountain had its god or nymph. The Celts threw precious objects into deep water to make contact with the divine presences of the underworld.

Buddhists seek enlightenment not in the sky above but in the mind within. 'What is Life? It is the flash of a firefly in the night. It is the breath of a buffalo in the winter time. It is the little shadow which runs across the grass and loses itself in the Sunset' wrote Crowfoot the Blackfoot Indian.[2] For Hindus not only cows but everything in nature is sacred. The *devas,* 'the shining ones', are the cosmic powers manifesting themselves in the natural forms of creation. But Brahman also reveals himself within the heart, as we read in the Upanishads. For Christians God took flesh. In *The Confessions* Augustine talks continuously to the God who dwells deep within his own being, 'God you who are the only true husbandman of that field which is our heart'.[3] More drily, Aquinas makes the same point in his *Summa Theologiae Pars Prima Quaestio 8* where he discusses the omnipresence of God. 'I answer that God is in all things....as long as a thing has being, God must be present in it according to its mode of being. But being is innermost in each thing and most fundamentally inherent in all things. Hence it must be that God is present in all things, and innermostly.'

* * *

If Darwin had pondered more deeply over where the inner variations that were the linchpin of his theory ultimately come from, then not only might he have contributed to the reconciliation of science and religion, he might have greatly illuminated religion's understanding of its own beliefs. Once you stop seeing species as fixed entities created once for all long ago, the way is open to contemplating a divine force actively and dynamically working deep in the universe. Where do the variations come from? The modern geneticists still cannot tell us. Are we really to believe that the glories of the organic world have arisen simply out of copying errors? This living, active dynamic presence of God in the world is the central teaching of all the mystics through the ages, both eastern and western. 'The world is charged with the grandeur of God' wrote Gerard Manley Hopkins. There is nothing in the facts that Darwin discovered that contradicts him. What a great mystical writer the man who wrote of his experiences many years before that 'the higher feelings of wonder, admiration and devotion bore irresistible testimony to God and the immortality of the soul' might have become. The tragedy of this immensely gifted religious poet who shrank into the miserable barnacle watcher of Darwin's middle age is pitiful. The loss to religion and to the nobility of the human spirit is incalculable.

Perhaps the deepest shadow of *The Origin* lies over the future. Darwin's replacement of love as the animating force of nature with competition and extermination gave licence to the ransacking of nature, and our lack of love and respect for it, that underlies our growing environmental crisis. His teaching in *The Descent of Man* that one only feels love for one's immediate circle undercut the universal sympathy of Adam Smith's *The Theory of Moral Sentiments.* If a globalized world in which resources are shrinking is to retain its humanity, it is Smith we need, not Darwin, or, at least, not the Darwin of *The Descent.* The confused thinking of *The Descent* and *The Origin* has contributed in no small part to the self-delusions of the western liberal myth that, more than anything else, are paralyzing our capacity to deal with climate change. Yet, ironically, if we wish to find inspiration to save the glories and beauties of the planet on which we live, it is to Darwin that we must turn, but to the young Darwin of *The Journal.* If *The Journal* had flowered into *The Origin,* what a light for mankind it would have been. Darwin's great book, his great gift to mankind, is not *The Origin.* It is *The Journal.*

(Endnotes)

1   See Robert Jay Lifton 1986 *The Nazi Doctors* ch 18
    'Healing-Killing Conflict: Eduard Wirths'. Basic Books.
2   *Touch The Earth* complied by T.C. McLuhan.
    London Abacus 1973
3   Augustine *Confessions* tr. E.M. Blaiklock. London
    Hodder & Stoughton 1983

Index

Index

Index

Index

Enjoyed this book?

Find out more about the author,
and a whole range of exciting titles at
www.discoveredauthors.co.uk

Discover our other imprints:

DA Diamonds traditional mainstream publishing

DA Revivals republishing out-of-print titles

Four O'Clock Press assisted publishing

Horizon Press business and corporate materials